Call of the Era

being the Change, through changing our Being

Kaye Twining

Tree of Life - Spiritual Practice Education for Today's World

www.treeoflifespirituality.com

Spiritual Wellbeing
The sacred work of being human

sit . . . wait . . . breathe in rhythm with the land

photo by Andrew Twining

Pioneer

Pioneer, driven to start afresh in a new land.

Sit . . . wait . . . breathe . . .
Breathe in rhythm with the land itself.
Listen . . . listen for the heartbeat.
Listen for the songline.
Sing . . .sing a new song.

Pioneer, invited to live afresh in a new land.

Kaye Twining

This book is dedicated to

Those who sense something is awry in the world.

Those seeking to be change agents, but are unsure where to start.

Those seeking a framework of understanding for our era of history.

Those intentionally seeking meaning and belonging in today's world.

Acknowledgements

I am grateful to those pioneers of inner change who have gone before us. They have perceived the Call of the era and have courageously undertaken the sacred work of pioneering a new collective *way of being* in the world. As such, they have shone light on a pathway for those of us who now follow in their footsteps.

My heartfelt gratitude goes to husband and partner in life, Andrew. His unending love, encouragement, and support for my work in the field of spiritual practice education has carried me through the highs and lows of such a venture.

Finally, to our children and grandchildren, thank you for your continuing love, support, inspiration, and willingness to challenge and expand my world view.

following the pathway of earlier pioneers of inner change

photo by Andrew Twining/Kaye Twining

Table of contents

Preface

Introduction

Call of the Era

What is the Call?
Responding to the Call
Recognizing the season
The Call and truth
The Call of this era
Summary

Living with Change

Change is a given of life
A lexicon of change
The winds of change
Opening the door to inner change
Conscious grieving
Impediments to inner change
Summary

Changing our Being

A symbol for inner change
Facing the limits
The good news
A new grounding principle
A new set of assumptions
A shift in identity
A new sacred narrative
A new song of belonging
Why bother?
Internarrative dialogue
Summary

Concluding remarks

Postscript
What is spirituality?

About the author

Resources

Copyright

Photo descriptions

Preface

A question had suddenly broken into my awareness. "What does it mean to be human in an evolving universe?" I could not shake it. The question demanded my attention. So, I allowed the question to work its way through me to completion. It took approximately sixteen years. During those sixteen years, I undertook a theological degree as a mature-aged student. Subjects included systematic theology, philosophy, history of world religions, human faith development, and the spirituality of Australian Indigenous people. Also during that time, I underwent a transformation of my *way of being* in the world. The transformation commenced with a personal crisis of meaning, where my concept of selfhood broke apart in response to ongoing lived experience. Beliefs which had once shaped my experience of identity and purpose no longer seemed tenable. I experienced inner disorientation. I was lost in terms of being and belonging. I remember journaling, "I feel myself fall . . . falling deeper, faster, down, down, down, into the darkness. I land with a thud on the cold, damp, rocky floor of the dark abyss of meaningless. I feel abandoned. I lay alone, in fetal position, in the darkness. Who am I, if not a child of the Father God?" My inner being had been wrenched apart. In response, I took the time to consciously grieve the loss of who I had known myself to be.

Once acclimatized to feeling lost, I chose to undertake an inner adventure of contemplative self inquiry toward discovering a new belief system, in the form of a sacred narrative which resonated with mind and heart . . . now. In short, I chose to engage in my personal transformative *dance* of being and becoming. I had expected such inner exploration to remain within the boundary of the religious tradition of my birth. Imagine my surprise when, after the many years of inner exploration, I awoke one day to the realization that I had been found; found within a new sacred narrative beyond the boundary of the religious faith tradition. At first I felt despair that my new sacred narrative no longer stood within a familiar landscape. And yet, I trusted the process of transformation which had led me there. Also, once the door to another *way of being* had opened, there was no option of turning back. Therefore, I chose to explore this new inner landscape. As a consequence, I had to consciously grieve the loss of belonging within a religious faith community.

So began a new inner adventure in the form of inhabiting a new inner landscape. It felt like I was living life afresh, in a completely new land. At the one time it felt both unsettling and exhilarating. Who would I know myself to be in this new land? How would this new inner landscape reshape my experience of belonging in the world? By way of responding to those questions I sought a language which gave expression to the transformation taking place within my inner being. Those explorations in language can be found on the Resources page at: www.treeoflifespirituality.com

Even though the religious tradition of my birth is no longer a place I call home, I am grateful to have lived into, from, and through that religious tradition. I continue to draw from its wisdom teachings. Now though, I feel at home in this new inner landscape. I once again *stand in my own ground - openheartedly*. I once again live daily life with integrity and authenticity. In short, I sing a new song of belonging.

During the course of my inner exploration toward a new song of belonging, I came across the work of cultural historian and ecophilosopher, the late Thomas Berry. Berry argued that Western culture was inbetween stories of being and belonging. Therefore, it was his contention that our era was calling for a new cultural sacred narrative, one which located our human identity within Life's 13.8-billion-year evolutionary history. Berry's notions of inbetween stories and generating a new story, captured my imagination. Why? Perhaps because of my own experience of having done just that. Perhaps also because his research responded somewhat to my question: "What does it mean to be human in an evolving universe?" Berry's research offered a framework of understanding for my own experience, while at the same time broadening my horizon toward the idea of cultural sacred narratives, within a larger Universe story. Berry was for me, one pioneer who shed light on the pathway of living into the Call of the era.

Berry was not alone in his naming of the era. I came across numerous authors who echoed Berry's sentiments including, Joanna Macy, Margaret J Wheatley, Barbara Marx Hubbard, Anne Hillman, Charles Eisenstein, and Duane Elgin. Each of those authors, in their own way, argued that Western societies were at a turning point. Turning points can be extremely disruptive. At the same time, author and spiritual mentor, Anne Hillman, maintained that transformation can take place at turning points. The transformation required in today's world involves a new cultural sacred narrative of being and belonging. Therefore, rather than a tinkering at the edges of the former narrative, our era is calling for deep change. Deep change, as claimed by author and change consultant, Robert E Quinn, refers to changing from "one set of deeply held assumptions to another set." Therefore, deep change starts from the inside . . . out. In line with such an understanding of deep change, today's world requires that we do the sacred work of generating a new set of assumptions for our collective *way of being* in the world. Transformation of assumptions is no easy task. The good news is that a new set of assumptions is emerging into conscious view. Consequently, our sacred work involves consciously attuning to that which is already emerging. If we choose to undertake such a sacred work, we will once again be able to collectively *stand in our own ground, openheartedly;* participating in the global community with integrity and authenticity.

This book presents the distilled essence of my many years of research and personal reflection on the Call of the Era, grounded by the question: "What does it mean to be human in an evolving universe?" Even though the book takes a large scale perspective, it is not intended to be a theory of everything. Rather, the book is offered into the public arena as an entry point for readers to engage with and reflect upon within the light of their belief system and lived experience. Hopefully the book will engender more questions than answers. Also, even though the research is drawn from a diverse range of sources, the lens for engaging with the sources is that of spiritual practice education. Spiritual practice education relates to meaning making, and the experience of belonging in the world. Furthermore, the book is designed with both artwork and language. The intention of such a design is to engage each reader's body, mind, will, and emotions, and in doing so, spark and support their own spirit of inquiry into the Call of the Era.

Kaye Twining
Bachelor of Theology, Graduate Diploma (Spiritual Direction), Master of Arts

Introduction

We humans long to experience belonging in our world. Yet, how can we experience belonging in an era characterized by the phrase, "all is not well in the world?" Daily the news media depicts graphic images of the effects of: the covid-19 pandemic; climate change; species extinction; global economic inequality; systemic racism; nonbinary gender fluid discrimination; institutional sexual abuse; family violence; growing numbers of refugee people; and the rise of religious and national fundamentalism. Within such a world, many people are experiencing a loss of belonging. Our world is crying out for change; change toward a more equitable world for all life forms. Yet, there can be no significant change in the *way we live* together without a change in our *way of being* in the world. Why? Because who we know ourselves *to be* at any given time and place, determines both our experience of belonging, and the way we act within our world. Therefore, if we are to make the necessary changes in the *way we live* together, we are required to change our *way of being* in the world. Consequently, alongside the Call for outer change is a deeper Call toward recasting our human identity; a change from the inside...out. How do we generate such inner change? In response, this book outlines foundational principles and practices for changing our human *way of being* in the world, with particular emphasis on the Western cultural identity.

The book is written in three chapters. The first chapter is entitled: Call of the Era. The chapter describes our desire to give meaning to our living and our dying, as well as our longing to belong. It situates such a desire and longing within the innate Call of belonging within the very nature of Life itself. We respond to such a Call through generating a belief system in the form of a meaningful sacred narrative; a belief system which responds to the particular Call of the era, and resonates with the minds and hearts of a majority of a given people, at a given time. A sacred narrative is generated through posing spiritual questions around meaning and belonging within the light of current scientific knowledge and beliefs regarding the origins of the universe, and the nature of reality. Such an understanding calls into question the nature of truth in relation to sacred narratives. This section also outlines the particular Call of our era.

The second chapter is entitled: Living with Change. The chapter outlines my exploration into the term *change*, commencing with a general description of the nature of change. From there, a lexicon locates the term *change* within the context of transformation. Following the lexicon, the chapter focuses on inner change, including pivotal moments of dramatic change; opening the door to inner change; the life affirming practice of conscious grieving; and finally noting some impediments to inner change.

The third chapter is entitled: Changing our Being. The chapter commences by offering a symbol - the labyrinth - for the process of inner change. The chapter continues by facing the limits of the assumptions which have orientated our experience of being and belonging. From there the chapter identifies a new context for reposing our spiritual questions. The new context involves a systems view of evolutionary history. Such a context gives rise to a new grounding principle of interconnectedness through unity with diversity, and a new set of assumptions which can orientate a new sacred narrative of being and belonging. A new sacred narrative locates the Western cultural identity and purpose within a greater Story of Life itself. The resulting shift in identity is from Self and life to *self-in-Life*. The chapter concludes with an exploration of internarrative dialogue.

The human heart longs to belong . . .
Yet if we cannot discover a shelter of belonging within our lives,
we can become a victim and target of our longing.

John O'Donohue
Eternal Echoes: Exploring our Hunger to Belong

Call of the Era

Being human within an evolving universe entails discovering our place of belonging within a given era. Such a sacred work draws us into an ever-deepening experience of connection in the here-and-now, while at the same time continuing to participate in Life's creative *dance* of being and becoming.

to experience belonging in the world, with joyful humility, trust, and reverence

photo by Haley Cornish/Kaye Twining

What is the Call?

Intrinsic to human experience is a yearning to belong. *Belonging* here refers to a deeply felt experience of connectedness within the three interrelated dimensions of human consciousness. The first dimension is within our own skin. In this dimension belonging can be experienced in the form of inner freedom and personal wholeness. The second dimension is within community. In this dimension belonging can be experienced in the form of authentic communal connection and response-ability. The third dimension is a greater Story of Life itself. In this dimension belonging can be experienced in the form of joyful humility, trust, and reverence for the mystery of participating in Life's creative *dance* of being and becoming. When we experience belonging in these three dimensions of human consciousness we feel at home in the world. When we feel at home in the world, we live daily life with integrity and authenticity.

Our yearning to belong does not sit within a vacuum. Rather, within the deeper rhythms of Life itself is an enduring Call of belonging. While such a Call of belonging remains constant throughout history, the shape of human belonging continues to change in each new era. So, the Call involves attuning our longing to belong with Life's particular Call of belonging at any given time and place in history. How do we experience Life's Call of belonging? According to Hillman, we perceive Life's "wordless" Call of belonging, in the form of an "ongoing inquiry into life." As a consequence, we humans are innately inquisitive. In keeping with Hillman, philosopher and theologian, the late Bernard Lonergan argued that we humans, "have the capacity to wonder, to pose questions, and discover responses." In line with such a spirit of inquiry, we have looked up into the night sky and wondered, "What is out there?" We have looked to the horizons of land and ocean and wondered, "What is beyond those horizons?" "We have looked at planet Earth and wondered, "What is it made of?" "How did it come to be?" And more recently, "What happens if Earth ceases to be habitable?" In response to our innate inquisitiveness, we humans are explorers. We continue to explore the lands, the oceans, the skies, and even deep space. Our desire to explore the various realms of the natural, or outer world, is the work of the sciences.

Beyond our curiosity regarding the outer world, we also have an innate curiosity regarding our inner world. Our curiosity in this regard takes form in questions such as: "Where did we come from?" "What is our purpose?" "What becomes of us when we die?" "Are we alone in the universe?" "How do we belong?" "Is there a god/s?" "Why is there good and evil in the world?" "What does it mean to be human in an evolving universe?" "What is the source and nature of love?" The exploration of our inner world is the work of spirituality. We do not, however, pose our spiritual questions within a vacuum. We pose them within the light of current scientific understandings of the origins of the world we inhabit, and the nature of reality. As a result, even though the sciences and spirituality are distinct disciplines of human endeavour, both disciplines assist us to discover and take up our place of belonging in the world.

The Call is to experience belonging in the world, at any given time and place in history.

a sacred narrative offers an *inner shelter of belonging*
within Life's creative *dance* of being and belonging

photo by Robert Tyzzer

Responding to the Call

In response to Life's enduring Call of belonging, and our human longing to belong, we are both driven and enabled to generate a belief system which authentically addresses our spiritual questions. Therefore, we respond to Life's Call of belonging by engaging in the sacred work of spiritual exploration. Because we pose our spiritual questions (as listed on the previous page) within the light of current lived experience and scientific knowledge, such experience and knowledge are both the lens through which we explore our spiritual questions, and the boundary of our perceptions. The responses discovered generates a unified belief system in the form of a sacred narrative. As with any narrative, a sacred narrative comprises a beginning, a middle, and an ending. The beginning responds particularly to the question: "Where did we come from?" The ending responds particularly to the question: "What becomes of us when we die?" The middle responds to the other questions listed on the previous page. Through a life affirming sacred narrative we know who we are, why we are here, and how we are to live. We become visible to ourselves and to each other. We gain a clear view of our collective identity and purpose. In line with such an understanding, scientific exploration gives rise to knowledge and beliefs about the world. Within the light of such knowledge, spiritual exploration enables us to experience meaning in the world via a sacred narrative. Consequently, the fabric of a sacred narrative is woven out of ongoing scientific and spiritual exploration.

In light of the above, a sacred narrative is meaningful when it attunes to the Call of the era, and resonates with the minds and hearts of a majority of people within a given society, at a given time. *Mind* here refers to a cultural world view. A cultural world view includes current scientific knowledge, as well as current societal norms, customs, rituals, socially acceptable behaviours, beliefs, religious and spiritual traditions, philosophical understandings, laws, and punishments for breaking such laws. When a sacred narrative is coherent with a cultural worldview, it offers a rational source for giving meaning. As such, sacred narratives are culturally embedded. *Heart* here refers to the ability of a sacred narrative to integrate the expected joys, sorrows, fears, angers, and frustrations of daily life as well as the unexpected traumas, and the peak unitive, or mystical, experiences. When a sacred narrative resonates with both mind and heart it becomes the rational means for giving meaning to our living and our dying.

What does a sacred narrative have to do with the experience of belonging? When our sacred narrative is coherent with the era, we experience what Celtic poet, the late John O'Donohue, named as an inner "shelter of belonging." Such an *inner shelter* offers a visceral experience of connectedness with self, others, and Life itself. The term *shelter* is important here. A physical shelter is a visible, often three-sided structure which is designed to temporarily protect those inside from the harsher elements of the natural world. A physical shelter may be well made, yet easily moveable. In a similar manner, an *inner shelter of belonging* enables us to become visible within the vast Story of Life itself. Otherwise, we may become disorientated, or completely lost in the immensity of Life's *dance* of being and becoming. An *inner shelter* has form in terms of authentic being-in-the-world. At the same time an *inner shelter* is open to shifts in the outer environment. Therefore, through an *inner shelter of belonging* we can experience authentic being and belonging in the present, while remaining open to transformative shifts in our view, if and when necessary.

cultural sacred narratives do break apart

In light of the previous page, we humans are storytellers. Since ancient times we have given meaning, and experienced belonging, through a sacred narrative. For example: the First Nations people of Australia who have inhabited the land for over 60,000 years. Their sacred narrative is: The Dreaming. Sacred narratives are essentially faith stories. Faith is often equated with religion; however a faith story may stand within one of the world religious traditions, but not necessarily so. Faith, in its most generic form, is a life force which both drives and enables each one of us to give meaning to our living and our dying. So, faith is not a belief system as such. Rather, in response to Life's Call of belonging, faith drives and enables us to generate a meaningful sacred narrative. In turn, we experience belonging in the world.

Sacred narratives do not remain static. Over the lifespan of a culture, the sacred narrative continues to develop in response to ongoing lived experience and continuing scientific exploration. Also, at certain junctures in a culture's history the knowledge gained through continued scientific exploration breaks through the understandings that had previously been taken for granted. In turn, such new knowledge can break apart the prevailing sacred narrative. For example: in the 16th-century Italian astronomer, Galileo, observed that it was actually the Earth which rotated around the sun, not the other way around. Such an observation stood in direct contrast to the commonly held belief of the time that Earth was the central point around which all else revolved. In response to such a commonly held belief, Christian doctrine had been formed regarding the centrality of the human in relation to God. Galileo's research contravened the commonly held belief, which in turn, contravened church doctrine. Galileo's research caused such an outrage, he was put under house arrest. He was imprisoned because his scientific exploration challenged a cultural/religious meaning making assumption of the time.

When a once meaningful sacred narrative has broken apart, the people are left *in the dark*, so to speak, in terms of giving meaning, and experiencing belonging. There is no longer an integrated source for spiritual wellbeing. O'Donohue argued that at such times, the people involved can, "become a victim and target of their longing." Why? Because the drive to belong is so powerful that it can cloud rational judgments and in turn give rise to feelings, thought patterns, behaviours, and relationships which do not serve the individual, the society, or the wider world. Consequently, if people cannot experience belonging through a meaningful sacred narrative, they may well seek belonging through damaging ways. Alternatively, the people may seek to numb their intrinsic longing to belong through addictions, which could range from drug and alcohol, to social media, to wealth creation, to an overconsumption of goods, or, food. Yet, there is another way to move through *the darkness*. When a sacred narrative has broken apart, the people involved undertake the sacred work of reposing their spiritual questions within the light of current lived experience and scientific knowledge. They then discover responses which hold true for the present time. Such is the sacred work of being human.

We respond to Life's enduring Call of belonging by generating a life affirming sacred narrative which attunes to the Call of the era, and resonates with mind and heart.

Recognizing the season

The poet, David Whyte, contended that our way of viewing ourselves in our world can be likened to either a "beautiful home," or a "prison." Drawing from such imagery, a sacred narrative can be likened to a beautiful home when it attunes to the Call of the era and resonates with the minds and hearts of the majority of the people. Within such a beautiful home, the people feel safe; the people feel visible to themselves, to others, and to Life itself. They experience a song of belonging. Conversely, a sacred narrative can become like a prison, when the people remain locked within one that is no longer coherent. Thus, sacred narratives cannot remain static. Rather, sacred narratives are required to undergo seasons of change. In response to each change of season, spiritual intention and practice differs somewhat.

Sacred narratives continue to cycle through the following three recognizable seasons:

1. One season is where the sacred narrative is coherent with current knowledge, beliefs, and lived experience. Therefore, it is like a beautiful home. Such a beautiful home may expand in response to changes in the outer environment, but it generally keeps a similar shape and appearance. Spiritual intention and practice here involve an ever-deepening embrace of current identity, purpose, values, and experience of belonging.

2. Another season is where cracks appear in the sacred narrative. The knowledge gained through continued scientific exploration begins to break through the understandings that had previously been taken for granted. In turn, the society at large experience inner disquiet and restlessness. If such cracks are fought against or simply patched up, the narrative may end up becoming like a prison. Spiritual intention and practice in this season involve tenderly and nonjudgmentally posing the open ended question: "are we being invited to surrender an attachment to an assumption, or particular belief, which has now become obsolete?"

3. The third season is where the sacred narrative has broken apart, giving rise to a collective experience of inner disorientation and displacement. At such times the society as a whole experience a crisis of meaning and belonging. Spiritual intention and practice here commence with the recognition that the prevailing narrative is no longer tenable, and then consciously grieving the loss. Spiritual exploration continues by way of reposing the spiritual questions in an open ended way, and living into the responses. Over time a new cultural sacred narrative will emerge. In this way, endings give way to new beginnings.

Cultural sacred narratives continue to cycle through seasons. In response, spiritual intention and practice involve recognizing and responding to the season.

truth is both subjective and objective

The Call and truth

As far as we know, we humans are the meaning making species of the Earth community. We do not, however, passively receive meaning. Rather, we give meaning through a coherent sacred narrative. A coherent sacred narrative is generated through reflection on, and subjective interpretation of, current scientific knowledge regarding the origins of the world we inhabit, the nature of reality, and our place of belonging within such understandings. Due to continued scientific exploration, our knowledge about the world continues to expand and evolve. In response, a sacred narrative necessarily changes over time? Furthermore, continued scientific exploration can give rise to additional spiritual questions. Thus, there are the time honoured spiritual questions, and time specific spiritual questions. For example: in response to scientific theories regarding evolution, a relatively new spiritual question is, "What does it mean to be human in an evolving universe?" Also, in response to technological advances, a spiritual question waiting on the horizon is, "What does it mean to be human in the light of artificial intelligence?" As a result of continued scientific and spiritual exploration, there can be no once-for-all-time sacred narrative.

The above understanding gives rise to the question: "What is the nature of truth in relation to sacred narratives?" Perhaps a sacred narrative is simply a fictional account of ourselves-in-life, constructed to make our living bearable. By way of responding to the question of truth, a sacred narrative is neither fiction, nor fact. Rather, a sacred narrative includes current facts about our world, our interpretation of such facts, and our response to our interpretation of such facts. As such, a sacred narrative is, in the words of Hillman "the compelling context" through which we give meaning to our lived experience; a compelling context derived through the rational exploration of our current knowledge about the world. Therefore, a sacred narrative cannot be an end-in-itself. Rather, a sacred narrative is the means through which we gain a clear view of identity, purpose, values, and belonging at any given time and place. As a result, the nature of truth in a sacred narrative is that it is both subjective and objective. How can truth be both subjective and objective? *Subjective* because the insights and understandings gained are interpreted and named through a particular world view. At the same time, when we do the inner work of posing our spiritual questions within the light of current understandings about Life itself, we experience what Lonergan named as, "objective truth." *Objective truth* here refers to understandings which have been tried and tested in life and found to hold true. Such understandings offer a rational foundation for our experience of belonging. So, when our sacred narrative is coherent with current knowledge, beliefs and lived experience, our sacred narrative offers an objective means for giving meaning and experiencing belonging . . . for now.

The truth is that giving meaning, and experiencing belonging, are subjective, because such endeavours are situated within a particular world view, at a particular time and place in history.

to continue to pioneer change from the inside . . . out

The Call of this era

Even though Life's Call of belonging remains constant throughout history, the shape of belonging continues to change. Therefore, in differing eras of human history, we are tasked with the sacred work of discovering and taking up our place of belonging for that era. Responding to such a Call invites each one of us to an ever-deepening experience of connection in daily life, while at the same time continuing to participate in Life's creative *dance* of being and becoming. So, just as there is no once-for-all-time sacred narrative, there is also no once-for-all-time experience of belonging. Our sacred narrative and subsequent experience of belonging is determined by the era of evolutionary history into which we are born. As presented in the Introduction, this current era is crying out for change in the *way we live* together, toward a more equitable world for all life forms. Therefore, global social change forms part of this era's Call of belonging. Yet, significant global social change requires a change of identity. Therefore, the deeper Call of the era is one of recasting our human *way of being* in the world.

Alongside this era's Call for global change, many authors have argued that Western civilization is at a turning point regarding its particular *way of being*. Turning points are disruptive. Turning points can be confronting, confusing, and disorientating. Turning points can also signal that a particular sacred narrative has run its course of usefulness. If it is true that Western civilization's sacred narrative is breaking apart, then the Call of the era would be one of consciously recasting the collective *way of being* through generating a new cultural sacred narrative. Such a change would involve more than a tinkering at the edges of the former narrative. It would involve a transformation of the assumptions which orientate the sense of collective identity. A new cultural identity would give rise to a new sense of purpose. A new sense of purpose would give rise to a new values system. A new values system would give rise to new *ways of living* together. Therefore, within the general Call of the era toward global change, sits the more particular Call for Western societies to recast their identity.

In light of the above, the Call of the era is to continue to pioneer change from the inside . . . out. Therefore, the Call is one of generating a new *way of being* in the world, through a new sacred narrative which is orientated around a new set of assumptions. Recasting our human identity in this way is no easy task. Nevertheless, we humans have successfully undertaken the venture previously, and will have to do so again in the future. It is the sacred work of being human. So, rather than being paralyzed by fear, or trying to squash our experience of belonging into a shape which is now obsolete, we can take heart that we are responding to the Call of the era by participating in an historical transformation of the human self concept.

The Call of this era is to change the *way we live* together, through recasting our *way of being*.

A Summary of the Call of the Era

We humans respond to Life's enduring Call of belonging by generating a meaningful, life affirming sacred narrative around identity and purpose. Such a sacred narrative determines our collective *way of being* in the world. When a sacred narrative responds to the particular Call of the era, and resonates with a majority of hearts and minds within a given society at a given time, the sacred narrative gives rise to an instinctual song of belonging. Therefore, a sacred narrative gives rise to the experience of spiritual wellbeing in the form of authentic being and belonging. Conversely, when a once meaningful sacred narrative breaks apart, there is no longer an integrated source for spiritual wellbeing. At such times, the longing to belong may drive people to unhealthy thoughts and actions.

Sacred narratives centre upon current understandings of the origins of the universe, the nature of reality, and our human place of belonging within such understandings. Therefore, sacred narratives do not remain static. Rather, sacred narratives continue to change in response to ongoing lived experience, and ongoing scientific exploration. Consequently, we humans are tasked with the periodic endeavour of re-narrating our collective identity and purpose. Such is the sacred work of being human.

In this era of Western cultural history, it would seem that the sacred narrative is breaking apart. With no functional sacred narrative in place, the people are left *in the dark* in terms of authentic being and belonging. Therefore, the particular Call of this era is to do the sacred work of spiritual exploration toward a new sacred narrative which can orientate a new *way of being* in the world. In short, the Call is one of changing from the inside . . . out. Even though the task ahead is challenging, the good news is that a new context for posing spiritual questions has emerged into conscious view. Therefore, the work involves consciously attuning to that which is already taking place in our world.

Living with Change

Change is natural and necessary to Life's creative *dance* of being and becoming.

Change, in the form of evermore complex stages of development, continues to take place within the three interwoven arenas of the natural world, cultural world views, and personal human experience.

set within Life's creative *dance* of being and becoming

Change is a given of life

Indian lawyer and nonviolent social activist, the late Mahatma Gandhi, advocated that we "be the change, we want to see in the world." Gandhi's words caught my attention, so I began to consciously live into *being* the change I wanted to see in the world. At first my emphasis was on the *being* part of the phrase. Then my attention was drawn to the *change* part of the phrase. So, this chapter outlines my exploration into the term *change*. To set the scene, the chapter commences with a general description of the nature of change, followed by a lexicon which situates the term *change* within the context of inner transformation. From there, the chapter focuses on inner change.

The nature of change

There are two givens in life - death and change. The autumn leaves (pictured opposite) characterize the two givens, in that the fallen leaves signify the death of a particular leaf as well as the seasonal cycle of change that a deciduous tree undergoes. In line with the example of the autumn leaves, it would seem that death belongs naturally with the cycle of change. Why are death and change a given? Because both are intrinsic to the evolutionary nature of Life itself, which science currently understands to be 13.8-billion-years in the making, thus far. *Evolution,* in this book, is named as Life's creative *dance* of being and becoming. According to author and integral philosopher, Steve McIntosh, such a *dance* involves ever more complex and integrated stages of development. Within the evolutionary process, it would seem that change and death are a natural and necessary part of the cycles and arcs of ongoing stage development. Consequently, we and the world we inhabit, continue to undergo death and change.

Change, in the form of stages of development, continues to take place in the three interwoven arenas of the natural world, cultural world views, and personal human experience. The following outlines how such stages of development are experienced. Firstly, the human experience. A baby is born. Then, if everything goes according to plan, the baby grows through childhood, adolescence, young adulthood, middle adulthood, elderhood, then death. In response to each stage of physical development, they will most likely experience a shift in their inner world; in their experience of being and belonging. Therefore, within the wider experience of the 13.8-billion-year evolutionary history, where death and change are a natural and necessary part of the process, each human being lives out their personal *dance* of being and becoming. *Being* here refers to: who they know their self to be at any given time and place in terms of identity, purpose, values, and belonging. *Becoming* refers to: transformative shifts in their view. The ongoing *dance* of being and becoming is intrinsic to the human experience of Life.

Secondly, the cultural experience. Cultural world views continue to undergo stages of development. For example: Western culture has undergone the stages of the ancient, the middle ages, the early modern, the modern, the postmodern, and now the post postmodern, or transmodern. Such stages of

each developmental stage is unique, necessary, and both included and transcended within the next stage

development have not taken place in a linear fashion toward a more perfected stage. Rather, each stage of development has involved an adaptation to Life as it is currently experienced. Alongside stages of development, cultures also have life spans. According to the field of life cycles of civilizations, all civilizations cycle through a pattern of "ascendency" through to "collapse." (See the research of Sir John Glubb as quoted by Margaret J Wheatley). According to the research, Western civilization is currently exhibiting signs of the collapse, or death, part of the pattern. Thus, within the wider experience of Life's creative dance of being and becoming, where death and change are both natural and necessary, cultures live out their own *dance*.

Finally, the natural world. Earth's evolutionary process of stage development has been named in the following geological stages: The Precambrian, The Palaeozoic, The Mesozoic, and the Cenozoic. Thomas Berry added the Ecozoic era to that list. Berry recognized a shift taking place from the Cenozoic era. In response, he coined the word Ecozoic, which is a prescriptive term for an emerging era which redefines the relationship between humans and the natural world, in terms of mutuality. Included in the natural world's process of evolutionary stage development are at least five mass extinctions which, according to Wikipedia comprised, "widespread and rapid loss of biodiversity." So again, death and change seem to be an integral part of Life's creative *dance* of being and becoming.

It is important to emphasize once again that in each of the three interwoven arenas of the natural world, cultural world views, and personal human experience, stages of development do not occur in a linear fashion, toward an end goal of perfection. Rather, each stage is a necessary adaptation within the evolutionary process of Life itself. As a result, later stages of development are not superior to former stages. Rather, each new stage of development both includes the former stages of development and transcends the limitations of the same. In this way, each stage of development is unique, authentic, and valuable in its own right, while also being part of a greater whole.

In light of the above, when we situate our personal human experience within the bigger picture of Life itself, we recognize that our living is permeated with change. *Change* here is contextualized within Life's evolutionary process of stages of development. Such stages of development are a necessary part Life's creative *dance* of being and becoming. Therefore, to live, is to live with change.

The term *change* is contextualized within Life's creative *dance* of being and becoming. Within such a context, change is both natural and necessary.

without formation there can be no transformation

A lexicon of change

This section comprises a further exploration of the term *change*. According to the Merriam-Webster Dictionary, synonyms for the term *change* include: alteration, difference, refashioning, remodelling, reviewing, reworking. A term akin to *change*, and one which can incorporate the synonyms as listed, is *transformation*. The term *transformation* can be broken down into: *trans* meaning - to go beyond; and *formation* meaning - something which has a discernible form, or shape. Therefore, trans-formation here means the potential to break through and transcend the limitations of a particular form. So, fundamental to the nature of transformation, is formation. Without formation, there can be no transformation. Consequently, both formation and transformation play their part in the *dance* of being and becoming. Within the confines of this book, the term *change* refers to the above understanding of transformation.

Change, in the shape of breaking through and transcending the limitations of a current formation, occurs within both the outer and the inner worlds. In terms of the outer world, evolutionary change usually takes place slowly over many, many years. Even so, there are also pivotal moments in *the dance* where a monumental leap takes place. In turn, the limitations of a particular formation are broken through and the formation is restructured. Author and public speaker, Barbara Marx Hubbard, cited one such evolutionary leap as the jump from single cell life forms which were restricted to living in the oceans, to multicellular life forms which could breathe on land. Such an evolutionary leap is thought to have taken place around 600 million years ago. Regarding such pivotal moments of change, Hubbard argued, "the nature of nature is to transform," especially when it, "hits a crisis of limits." Both of those phrases by Hubbard resonated deeply within my inner being. As I continued to reflect on those two phrases I felt a sense of hope wash over me. All is not lost. Yes, planet Earth is moving toward a crisis of limits, but that is not the end of the story. Yes, the Western *way of living* has hit a crisis of limits, but that also is not the end of the story. Transformation on both counts is possible.

In terms of the inner world, formation refers to both our personal and collective *way of being* in the world. Therefore, formation relates to our experience of identity, purpose, values, and belonging. Our personal formation does not emerge within a vacuum. Rather, our personal formation is shaped by the collective formation. The collective formation is shaped by the current cultural world view. As mentioned previously a cultural world view is formed by current norms, knowledge, and beliefs. A cultural world view is, in the words of Lonergan, like an "horizon of meaning" which both shapes and limits all that we can "see, hear, and know" in the world. Lonergan went as far as to argue, "what does not fit into our horizon of meaning will not be seen or heard, or if it is, will be deemed as irrelevant." In this way, our world view acts as the interpretive framework for our experience of formation. Therefore, without a cultural world view there would be no foundation for generating a coherent sacred narrative of being and belonging. And yet, cultural world views can also hit "a crisis of limits."

a collective *way of being* can dissolve into mush

photo by Hayley Cornish

As with outer change, inner change usually takes place gradually in response to new knowledge and beliefs which expand the cultural world view. At the same time, there are pivotal moments within a culture's history when their world view is dismantled by the knowledge, beliefs, and lived experience of the time. In turn, the once meaningful sacred narrative is rendered obsolete, and as such, hits a crisis of limits. At such pivotal moments it is as if the collective *way of being* dissolves into mush, much like a caterpillar which turns to mush within its cocoon.   But that is not the end of the story. The form of a caterpillar has to turn to mush before the imaginal cells can start their work of transforming the mush into a moth or butterfly. The resultant moth or butterfly is not a superior form to that of the caterpillar, simply different. In a similar manner, when the collective *way of being* has turned to mush, the people of the culture are required to do the sacred work of imagining a new *way of being,* one which breaks through and transcends the limitations of the former way. The new *way of being* is not superior to the former way, simply authentic to the era. In time, the new *way of being* will hit its own crisis of limits.

Numerous authors have claimed that Western culture is experiencing such a pivotal moment in time. For example:

1.   Cultural historian and ecophilosopher, the late Thomas Berry claimed that we were inbetween stories. He contended that our mission was to renarrate the human identity at the level of species.
2.   Environmental activist, author, and scholar of general systems theory and deep ecology, Joanna Macy, named our time as, "the Great Turning;" turning from an "Industrialized Growth Society" to a "Sustainable Society."
3. Scholar of organizational behaviour, and author, Margaret J Wheatley, argued that Western culture was in the collapse part of its life cycle.
4.   Spiritual mentor and author, Anne Hillman argued that we were, "living in a great hinge of time in which everything is changing."
5. Public speaker and author, Charles Eisenstein, maintained that Western culture was shifting from a "Story of Separation" to a "Story of Reunion."

It would seem that our era is one of the pivotal moments in Life's creative dance which call forth dramatic change.

While the term *change* refers to both outer and inner transformation, the focus of this book is inner transformation. At this point in Western cultural history, inner transformation requires more than a change in perspective. Inner transformation requires that we figuratively, *see with new eyes*.

squalling beyond, among, and within, causing unrest

The winds of change

In our era, the winds of change are squalling incessantly. The winds of change are squalling beyond, among, and within, causing unrest in the natural world, unrest in the Western cultural world view, and unrest within individuals who hold the world view. It is as if a *perfect storm*, so to speak, has been generated. Factors contributing to the current *perfect storm* are: 1. No functional sacred narrative for personal or collective identity, purpose, values, and the experience of belonging. In turn, western societies are experiencing a collective crisis of meaning. 2. The covid-19 global pandemic which is causing millions of deaths across the globe, as well as economic disruption and challenges to social norms; 3. Climate change, which is causing more dramatic weather events, more often; 4. The threat of mass extinction of species; 5. An economic system which relies on unending expansion, no matter the cost to Earth's wellbeing; 6. Rising numbers of people forced to seek refuge in lands other than their own; 7. An information overload via the internet on social media platforms, which can be confusing at best and overwhelming at worst; 8. A global economic system geared toward the rich getting richer; 9. Terrorism, or the threat of terrorism, creating generalized anxiety, and suspicion of certain cultural and religious groups; 10. Familial and institutional sexual abuse highlighted by the *me too* movement; 11. Nonbinary gender fluid discrimination; 12. The insidious nature of family violence; 13. Systemic racism as highlighted by the global *black lives matter* movement; 14. Rising numbers of people, especially young people, presenting with anxiety and depressive disorders; 15. Large numbers of people who are homeless. In light of all these factors, today's world is crying out for a change in the cultural structures which sustain and contribute to the inequitable nature of the *way we live* together. Our era is calling forth major societal change.

If our era is calling forth major societal change, why does this book focus on change from the inside . . . out? Why focus on changing our *way of being* in the world? Well, as mentioned previously our identity determines our social structures. As a result, without a change in who we know ourselves to be, there will be no real change in our social structures. We can choose to deny, or fight against, such inner change. Perhaps the backlash of extreme right wing and white supremacist movements are expressions of fighting against the inner change required. Yet, for the necessary structural change to occur, it will require an inner change; a change of identity.

Our era is calling for social change toward a more equitable world for all life forms. Yet, there will be no substantial social change without a change in our human identity.

opening the door to inner change

photo by Robert Tyzzer

Opening the door to inner change

We cannot force, manipulate, or control the process of inner change toward a new identity. Neither is there a ten-step plan to reach a desired destination. Also, there is no clear pathway to follow. Rather, the pathway of inner change is known as the pathless path. As such, we can only see where the pathway has led, when we reflect back on our experience. How then do we engage in the process of transforming our *way of being* in the world? Remembering that inner change is undertaken in response to Life's Call of belonging, our task is to figuratively, *open the door*. *Opening the door* here refers to conscious intentionality. Conscious intentionality involves both remaining open to the possibility of transformative shifts in our *way of being*, and allowing the process of transformation to work its way through us in its own way and own time. The following elements enable us to *open the door* to transformative shifts:

Recognizing where we are

Within the gentling light of lovingkindness, we are required to take the time to recognize where the sacred narrative stands in terms of the cycle of seasons. In the matter of present day Western culture, it would seem that the sacred narrative is undergoing a season of breaking apart. Such a recognition can be unpleasant, even unnerving. At the same time, acceptance of such a recognition can offer a sense of release. Finally, we can understand why our world seems to be going awry. Also, acceptance of what is taking place, opens the door to what is possible. In this way acceptance gives rise to hope, in the form of the possibility of transformation, grounded in reality. One further reason why recognition is crucial, is that it enables us to choose which area of spiritual exploration is necessary at this time. (See: Recognizing the Season in the previous chapter).

A beginner's mindset

Inner change requires a beginner's mindset. According to the Zen Buddhist tradition, a beginner's mindset is one that is curious, patient, and receptive to what is, rather than a construction of what we would like to see. Through a beginner's mindset, we undertake the inner adventure of transforming our collective *way of being* in the world, without knowing the final destination.

A beginner's mindset does not require us to become a *blank slate*, so as to speak. Our task is to repose our spiritual questions within the light of current knowledge, beliefs, and lived experience. In that way, we do employ our intellect. Where the beginner's mindset comes in, however, is in allowing responses to emerge in their own way and own time. Therefore, we are required to put our attention on the questions and let the responses take care of themselves.

Spiritual exploration grounded by a contemplative orientation

Indian social activist and spiritual teacher, the late Vimala Thakar, claimed that intellectual theories cannot yield transformation because they are like maps of the terrain, rather than the terrain itself. Therefore, even though a theoretical appreciation of inner change is important, that alone is not enough. We are required to actually undertake the sacred work of spiritual exploration. Spiritual

"we build the bridge as we walk on it" Robert E Quinn

exploration is grounded by a contemplative orientation. A contemplative orientation involves a gentle, yet courageous intention to attune to inner wisdom's present moment stirrings toward authentic self discovery. Attunement involves deep listening. Deep listening requires an attitude of inner quietness and patience. Deep listening also involves vulnerability, in terms of remaining open to where inner wisdom may be guiding. Remaining vulnerable to the process involves trust. How may we learn to trust the process? We take tentative steps initially, then test the soundness of where those steps have led. How may we perceive inner wisdom's stirrings through a beginner's mindset and a contemplative orientation? Inner wisdom is perceived in the form of inklings, waves of impressions, images, words or phrases, and insights which seem to emerge from our inner depths. Thus, intellectual theories reside metaphorically, *in the head,* while a contemplative orientation resides metaphorically *in the gut.*

Spiritual exploration which is grounded by a contemplative orientation includes three particular elements. The first element involves relinquishing the desire to control the process of self discovery. Therefore, the inner adventure is undertaken, without knowing its duration, or, its final destination. In this regard, Quinn offered a helpful metaphor: "we build the bridge as we walk on it." Relinquishing the desire to control the process enables us to remain comfortable with the unknown, until it is known. The second element involves a receptive disposition. A receptive disposition involves an attitude of nonjudgmental curiosity. The third element involves the awareness of the gentling light of lovingkindness. Without lovingkindness, the process can become too intense, leading toward self annihilation. Self annihilation is not the intention of inner change. Rather, inner change is a life affirming spiritual practice toward once again embracing authentic formation, without attachment to a fixed identity.

In light of the above, spiritual exploration of our inner world involves a tender, yet courageous, process of noticing and attending to whatever is emerging into present moment conscious awareness. Regarding present moment awareness, O'Donohue, cautioned that our inner world, "was never meant to be seen completely." Consequently, he suggested that we approach our inner world through the metaphor of *candlelight*. He maintained that a candle shed enough light to, "befriend the darkness," and in so doing, disclose only that which requires attention at this time. Therefore, contemplative spiritual exploration focuses on that which is rising to the surface of our awareness in the present moment.

Open ended questions
The poet, Rilke urged us to love the questions and take the time to live into the responses. It took me sixteen years to live into my spiritual question, "what does it mean to be human in an evolving universe?" Living into the responses means that we do not try to force or manufacture answers. Rather, we undertake our research, go about our daily lives, and wait; wait for responses to emerge within us. Why do we have to wait? Remember that Lonergan asserted that our world view filters all that we can

open ended questions clear a pathway for inner change

see, hear, and know. As such, our world view is the boundary of what we can see and understand. We cannot see and understand responses which lay beyond the boundary of our current world view. Therefore, conditions need to be sufficient within us, before responses can emerge into our awareness. So we wait for conditions to be sufficient. When responses do emerge within our awareness, we are required to test them out. In this way we figuratively, *try them on to see how they fit*.

In a similar manner to Rilke, Lonergan's research into human consciousness brought him to the conclusion that open ended questions lay at the very heart of the transformative process. Why? Firstly, a spirit of inquiry is intrinsic to human consciousness. Therefore, we each possess an ability to pose open ended questions, and discover responses. Secondly, open ended questions can break through the boundaries of a world view. So, open ended questions are integral to the practice of spiritual exploration. The tone of the questioning, however, is critical. If the tone is one of open, patient, rational curiosity - and even a sense of playfulness - then transformative shifts are able to break through into our awareness. On the other hand, if our tone is one of probing, dissecting, or analyzing, the transformative process is inhibited. Therefore, the tone of the questioning is paramount.

Being attentive to our affective experience

Open ended spiritual questions clear a pathway for inner change. How though do we enable our questions to work their way through us to completion? Well, we pose our open ended questions within the light of current knowledge, beliefs and lived experience. Then we remain attentive to whatever affective, or felt, experience emerges in response. Lonergan argued that it was affective experience, rather than beliefs, that drove authentic self knowledge. Therefore, present moment affective experience becomes the entry point for further exploration toward perceiving new insights. Affective experience includes our emotions, for example: our joys, sorrows, angers, fears, and frustrations. In addition to such emotions, our affective experience also involves bodily sensations, and thoughts. *Thoughts* here refers to both that which arises in response to our spiritual exploration, and that which we can imagine to be possible. Noticing and becoming curious about present moment affective experience is a way of perceiving inner wisdom's stirrings through a whole of body experience.

In summary, we consciously *open the door* to inner change by: recognizing where we are; a beginner's mindset; spiritual exploration grounded by a contemplative orientation; open ended questions; and engaging with present moment affective experience.

We need not fear, nor fight against inner change. We can take comfort and inspiration from the knowledge that we are not in control of the process. We are, however, required to open the door.

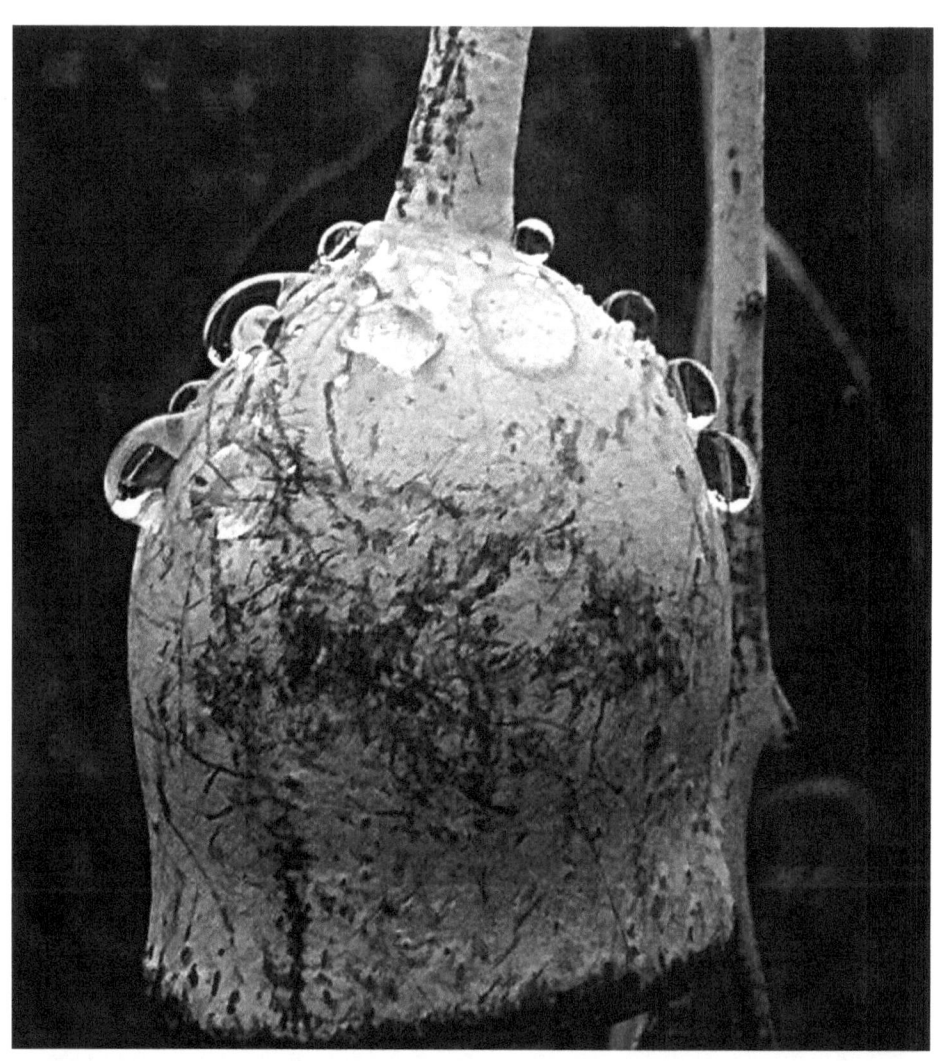

conscious grieving can play a purposeful role

Conscious grieving

The transformative process of inner change toward a new cultural identity takes us on a thrilling inner adventure. Yet, not all aspects are pleasant. We undertake the venture without knowing the destination, therefore the uncertainty of the venture can be quite daunting. Also, the prospect of getting lost in the questions is a real possibility. Furthermore, we are required to let go of a once meaningful song of belonging, which can give rise to an experience of loss. A healthy response to loss is to grieve, to consciously grieve. Even though conscious grieving cannot change the circumstances which gave rise to the experience of loss, conscious grieving can transform the way we identify with, or are defined by, the experience of loss. Therefore, conscious grieving is also an element within the process of inner change.

Author and clinical psychologist, Sameet M Kumar, argued that conscious grieving had a "purposeful" role to play in our lives. Conscious grieving becomes purposeful when it enables us to firstly respect the affective experience grief. Then, when appropriate, conscious grieving enables us to engage with the affective experience toward reframing the experience of loss into one of meaning. Within the context of this book, such a reframing is toward a new song of belonging. Conscious grieving can allow us to notice, express, explore, and integrate our emotions of grief in a healthy way. Even though conscious grieving is purposeful, it can be feared that if the flood gates of grief are opened, we will be swept away by them. Yet, it takes a massive amount energy to metaphorically *run-a-way, hide from, or numb* the emotions of grief. Therefore, even though it may seem counterintuitive, the spiritual practice of accepting and gently engaging with the emotions of grief, can offer a form of relief. Consequently, conscious grieving has little chance of emotionally overwhelming us. As such, conscious grieving is a life affirming spiritual practice, particularly relevant to the process of inner change.

In relation to changing the Western cultural identity, conscious grieving may also require engagement in a process of forgiveness; seeking forgiveness from others, and offering forgiveness to ourselves. This is especially so, when the former cultural sacred narrative enabled us to collectively use and abuse the natural world and many peoples, particularly First Nations people. Seeking forgiveness for such actions, as a form of inner healing, will enable us to truly live afresh in our world. Forgiveness is often viewed as weakness, but forgiveness requires of us resilience, courage, wisdom, and compassion. As such, forgiveness is not for the faint-hearted. The practice of seeking forgiveness does not remove all the pain. So, as we begin to engage with the process, the pain does not automatically disappear. The pain, however, does become bearable. In the light of such understandings, the intention of forgiveness is inner healing in the form of wholeness. Wholeness is not about hiding from certain aspects of ourselves, but bringing them into the gentle light of lovingkindness, and allowing our experience of them to be redeemed.

Conscious grieving can restore wholeness. Grounded by an experience of wholeness, rather than deficit, we can engage in the process of changing our *way of being* in the world.

inner change is possible in our era, but not a given

Impediments to inner change

Inner change is possible in our era, but not a given. There are numerous reasons why people may deny, or fight against, inner change. The following are some of those reasons:

Fear - We humans seek comfort and security. Change gives rise to uncertainty. Uncertainty gives rise to anxiety and fear.

Pride - We like to think we are in control of our destiny. It can be an affront to realize that our being and our doing are determined by a world view and a sacred narrative. Also, the need for ultimate truth is high in Western thought. So, the knowledge that our living is governed by a subjective sacred narrative can be unnerving.

Greed - Numerous nations, corporations, and individuals are profiting economically from the current cultural *way of being* in the world. They have no desire for change.

Lack of knowledge* or *understanding - Many people do not know that sacred narratives are culturally embedded. Also, that sacred narratives undergo seasons of change. In terms of present-day Western culture, how often do people sit around talking about the problems of our era, then shrug their shoulders, sigh, and say, "oh well, what can we do?"

Feeling lost - Some people choose to engage, but get lost in the questions. Life then takes on a meaningless quality.

Anger - Living through a time of inner cultural collapse can give rise to intense feelings of anger around questions like, "Why don't people just wake up and change?" "What's wrong with them?" Anger can lead some people to separate from society and live *off-the-grid*, so to speak.

Loneliness - Even though many individuals across the globe have begun the venture of inner change, it is still somewhat counter cultural. Therefore, it can feel like we are each undertaking the venture on our own.

Social Activism - many social activists rightly work toward structural change in the *way we live together*. Yet, social activism alone will not yield the necessary change. Without a change in identity, there will not be significant structural cultural change.

When we are aware of the impediments, we are able to transcend them.

A summary of living with change

Our era is characterized by the squalling winds of change which are sweeping through both the outer and inner worlds. While acknowledging that change is occurring in both worlds, this book focuses primarily on inner change; on the transformation of our human identity. Change can unnerve the human psyche. So, how can we live well with change? Understanding something of the nature of change in today's world can be beneficial. *Change* here is known to be a natural and necessary part of the evolutionary process; of Life's creative *dance* of being and becoming toward evermore complex stages of development. Each stage of development is unique and essential in its own right. At the same time, each stage of development is part of the greater whole of that which has gone before, and that which is yet to be. While change continues to take place gradually, there are pivotal moments in the *dance* when the change can be dramatic. In terms of cultural evolution, it seems that Western culture is undergoing such a pivotal change. Therefore, alongside a general global call for change, today's era is particularly calling for change in the Western *way of being* in the world.

There is no predetermined pathway for inner change. Rather, in response to Life's Call of belonging, we are required to consciously *open the door* for transformative shifts to emerge within our personal and collective awareness. We *open the door* through recognizing where we are; a beginner's mindset, spiritual exploration grounded by a contemplative orientation; posing open ended questions; engaging with present moment affective experience; and conscious grieving. Such a process draws from and flows back into daily life. Because of the many impediments to inner change, transformation of our human identity is possible, but not a given.

Changing our Being

To be the change we want to see in the world, requires that we change our *way of being* in the world.

one path which leads from the outer edges into the centre, then back out again

A symbol for inner change

The labyrinth has once again been reclaimed as both spiritual practice and symbol. As a symbol for inner change, the labyrinth represents a venture from our outer world, to the centre of our inner world, then back out again. Such a venture is undertaken in response to Life's enduring Call of belonging. The outer world comprises *the shallows* of daily life. The centre of our inner world comprises *the deep*, or our innermost orientating reference point. A labyrinth is not to be confused with a maze. A maze is designed to challenge the intellect, therefore dead ends are part of the plan. In contrast, a labyrinth has but one path which leads from the outer edges into the centre, then back out again. The twisting and turning of the path can sometimes leave travellers feeling momentarily disorientated. Even so, if the path is followed, it will safely return the travellers back home again. In like manner to a labyrinth, the pathless path of spiritual exploration toward inner change starts and ends with the outer edges, or *the shallows* of daily life. Why? Because we are not called to make our home in *the deep*. We are called to make our home in *the shallows* of daily life - on the other side of *the deep*.

In terms of a symbol for inner change, the inward path of the labyrinth represents the spiritual work of each traveller firstly being drawn to take their first step. Then further steps along the pathway comprise the noticing, expressing, and exploring of open ended questions, and resultant present moment affective experience. As necessary, each traveller undertakes the spiritual work of detaching from now outmoded beliefs and assumptions. Travellers then pause at the centre. Such an interior pause is not a passive stance. The interior pause involves each traveller choosing to surrender the desire to simply think their way through the process. Rather, they take the time to attune to inner wisdom's stirrings within them. Furthermore, the interior pause offers a time of inner rest, as each traveller chooses to consciously breathe in accord with the deeper rhythms of Life itself. Then, when travellers are ready, the interior pause offers a time for them to recognize and discern new insights emerging within the depths of their being. So, the interior pause is an integral part of engaging in the sacred work of inner change.

After the pause at the centre, the outward path of the labyrinth represents both the integration of the new insights into daily life, and the celebration of the same. When travellers reach the outer edge once again, they experience something of what poet T.S. Eliot expressed in The Four Quartets, in that spiritual exploration in response to Life's enduring Call of belonging enables each traveller to *re-turn home* to daily life, and experience *home* as if for the first time.

We are Called to live in *the shallows* of daily life, on the other side of *the deep*.

working against Life's creative *dance* of being and becoming

Facing the limits

Our Western *way of being* in the world seems to have hit its limits; hit a boundary that demands change. There are two particular reasons for making such a claim. The first reason is that our present *way of being* in the world no longer offers meaning or belonging. Why? Because the sacred narrative which formed our *way of being* no longer resonates with the collective mind and heart of Western societies. Consequently, our experience of identity and purpose has figuratively *turned to mush*. We no longer know who we are, why we are here, or how we are to live. We have lost our way. We no longer experience a song of belonging. The second reason that our *way of being* has hit a boundary that demands change, is because the previous sacred narrative gave rise to a values system which sought the flourishing of the individual, or select privileged groups, over all else. Such a values system contributed to the kind of abuses mentioned previously in the book. In terms of climate change, such a values system seems to be actually working against Life's creative dance of being and becoming. Therefore, the current values system is no longer tenable. Regarding climate change it is important to note the controversy around the cause. Opinions range from: "climate change has nothing to do with humanity" to "humanity is directly responsible for the current climate change." Perhaps the truth lay somewhere inbetween. Perhaps the current climate change is both part of an evolutionary process, and partly due to our current values system. Whatever the case, the previous sacred narrative has hit a boundary that demands change. In turn, there is now no functional sacred narrative from which to generate authentic being and doing. It is time to once again *open the door* to inner change in the form of recasting our human identity. It is time to once again *walk the labyrinth*.

Before we can begin to imagine a new *way of being*, it is important to understand the assumptions of the previous sacred narrative, and the context which contributed to such assumptions. If we are not aware of them, they may continue to unwittingly shape our view, thus thwarting the deep inner change required.

The former assumptions
The assumptions which orientated the previous sacred narrative included: anthropocentrism, tribalism, white supremacy, individualism, capitalism, and consumerism. Anthropocentrism refers to the primacy of the human species over and above all other species. Such an assumption gave rise to the perception that the human species was the centrepoint on which all life turned. Tribalism refers to the rigid boundaries of conformity which separate the various sub-groups within Western societies. Rigid boundaries offer clear lines of demarcation for who is in and who is out. White supremacy refers to the primacy of white skinned people over and above all other skin colours. Individualism refers to the primacy of the individual over and above the collective. Capitalism, according to the Oxford Dictionary, refers to "an economic and political system in which a country's trade and industry are controlled by private owners for profit, rather than the state." Consumerism refers to the concept that happiness depends upon continued accumulation of goods and services. Each one of these assumptions orientated our *way of being* in the world.

The context which contributed to the former assumptions
The context which contributed to the former assumptions included a particular science-based evolutionary theory of creation, and a mechanistic view of the nature of reality. In terms of the evolutionary theory of creation, such a theory involved a 13.8-billion-year process, and included a dead universe hypothesis. In terms of time frame, it is acknowledged there are numerous science-based time frames for the evolution of the universe, however, 13.8-billion-years seems to be the one more commonly accepted. Regarding the dead universe hypothesis, Duane Elgin argued that it was assumed that the universe was an "inhospitable place, comprised almost entirely of non-living matter and empty space." Furthermore, that creation was an once off event occurring, "billions of years ago when a massive explosion spewed out lifeless material debris into equally lifeless space." A dead universe hypothesis gave rise to the notion that we lived in an indifferent and meaningless universe, and as such, our lives were also meaningless. In response, one way we chose to fill the collective meaningless void was to gain a sense of control over our lives by dominating and exploiting those we considered *other*, including the world we inhabit. Another way we have filled the collective void of meaninglessness was by consuming as much as we could while we could, without measuring the cost to future generations.

In addition to the evolutionary, dead universe hypothesis, the second feature which contributed to the assumptions of the previous narrative was a mechanistic model for viewing the nature of reality. In a nutshell, a mechanistic model viewed reality in the form of an inanimate machine, with separate, independent components working together, until some part broke down. Then the task was to fix the broken part. In turn, scientific exploration was based on separating the component parts of life, then studying each component part in isolation from the whole. The mechanistic model gave rise to much knowledge regarding the structure and composition of the world and the human body/mind. At the same time, the mechanistic model gave rise to an either/or paradigm of adversarial dualistic opposites. For example: good Vs bad, positive Vs negative, white Vs black, matter Vs spirit, man Vs woman, science Vs religion, us Vs them, competition Vs cooperation. Within such an either/or construct, the motivating force of the evolutionary survival imperative was known to be: a competitive survival of the fittest.

The context of a mechanistic model and an evolutionary dead universe hypothesis, gave rise to the grounding principles of separation, independence, and domination. In turn, such grounding principles gave rise to judgment, fear, and prejudice toward those viewed as *other*. Also, within the light of such understandings of the origins of the universe and nature of reality, spiritual exploration was bound by the notion that we were separate, independent beings in competition with each other.

One further limitation of the previous sacred narrative
The previous Western sacred narrative was characterized by a dominant singular belief system, or storyline, to which all must adhere if they sought to belong. And yet, we now live in an era characterized by an image of the *global village*. The global village has emerged through the increase of overseas travel and the ease of communication across the globe via the internet. The global village has given rise to a spiritual expansiveness. In this regard, philosopher Ken Wilber argued that we are, "living in a time when all of the world's cultures and religious/spiritual traditions are available to us." In turn, there is an information overload of seemingly competing spiritual practices and belief systems to draw from. We truly are living in a spiritually expansive world. Such a spiritual expansiveness has challenged the former sacred narrative, which was centred primarily on the teachings of a culturally embedded Western Christian tradition. Now, we are living in an era which seeks meaning beyond a singular source, beyond a singular truth in the way we collectively give meaning to our living and our dying. Therefore, a new cultural sacred narrative will of necessity have to include multiple belief systems, rather than a dominant, singular storyline.

In light of the global village image, assumptions, and grounding principles as presented, it is no wonder that our *way of being* has hit a boundary which demands change. Such an understanding can be a rude, but necessary, awakening. So, where to from here? We are required to consciously grieve the loss of the previous sacred narrative, and the consequences arising from such a narrative. Then we are required to undertake the sacred work of spiritual exploration toward discovering a new *way of being* for our era. As we undertake such a task, we are consciously engaging in the sacred work of being human.

As confronting as it is to acknowledge, we have gone as far as we can with the assumptions and grounding principles of the former sacred narrative. They no longer serve us, or, the world we inhabit.

a systems view of evolutionary history

The good news

The good news is that we are no longer left *in the dark* in terms of a context for engaging in spiritual exploration. A new context has emerged. Therefore, there is reason for hope. Remember that the term *hope* means the possibility of inner transformation, grounded in reality. A new context is: a system's view of the 13.8-billion-years of evolutionary history. A systems view shifts the dead universe hypothesis to a living universe one. According to Elgin, "a living universe is a unified and completely interdependent system that is continuously regenerated by the flow-through of a phenomenal amount of life energy." In a similar vein, Indian-American physician and author, Deepak Chopra, wrote in the forward of Elgin's book: "the universe is conscious, self-regulating, self-creating, ever-renewing and always evolving to increasing levels of complexity and creativity." Within such an understanding of the evolutionary process, creation was not a one time event billions of years ago. Rather, creation involves an ongoing, moment by moment venture of which we humans are a part. So, even though the evolutionary time frame of 13.8-billion-years remains consistent, the view of Life's creative process has shifted dramatically.

A systems view

As well as shifting the creation theory from a dead universe to a living universe, a systems view has also shifted the nature of reality from a mechanistic model. In a nutshell, a systems view sees the fundamental nature of reality as *relationship*. In turn, the whole is known to be greater than the sum of the parts, because of the relationship between the parts. Furthermore, due to the nature of relationship, when one part is changed, the whole is changed in some way. Therefore, scientific exploration involves taking the whole into account and then seeking the relationships between the parts. If there is a break down in some way, the task is to look at what is causing the relationship to break down. So, a systems view does not invalidate previous scientific discoveries. Rather, a systems view transcends the limitations of a mechanistic view of reality.

In light of such an understanding of relationship, the universe is known to be a living system, made up of systems within systems; each system comprising a whole made of its own parts, while also being part of a greater whole. No particular system takes priority over another. For example: Earth is both a whole system in itself, with many parts, while also being part of a Solar System. In this way, a systems view shifts away from the either/or paradigm of the mechanistic model, toward a both/and paradigm. For example: both good and bad, both positive and negative, both black and white, both matter and spirit, both man and woman, both science and religion, both us and them, both competition and cooperation. In terms of a both/and paradigm, social psychologist, Diamuid O'Murchu maintained that each system has both a "self-assertive desire to preserve its own autonomy" and "an integrative tendency to function as part of the whole." Within such a construct, the motivating force of the survival imperative is known to be: interrelatedness through participation and cooperation.

A systems view gives rise to a paradigm of both/and. Such a paradigm is imbued with the notion of interrelatedness through participation and cooperative relationships.

a systems view welcomes difference

A new grounding principle

Within the light of a systems view of evolutionary history, where the fundamental nature of reality is known to be relationship, our collective inner orientating reference point is recast. Now, the grounding principle for a new song of belonging becomes one of: interconnectedness through unity with diversity. Intrinsic to such a principle are the qualities of participation and cooperation. The grounding principle of interconnectedness through unity with diversity, breaks through and transcends the principles of separation, independence, and domination, which were embedded in the previous sacred narrative.

Interconnectedness through unity with diversity
At the heart of the principle of interconnectedness through unity with diversity is the understanding that all life forms are interdependent within a framework of systems within systems. In terms of the human experience of systems within systems, we each know ourselves to be part of the one human species, without sacrificing our uniqueness; our individual uniqueness (personal self systems), our cultural uniqueness (collective systems of shared norms and beliefs). In this regard, scholar of general systems theory, Joanna Macy, argued that unity with diversity, "does not sacrifice, but instead requires the uniqueness of each part." Consequently, unity is no longer bound within the construct of uniformity, where sameness is paramount. Neither does unity involve tolerating difference. Even though tolerance takes a step beyond the principle of domination, the idea of tolerating difference is based in the previous principles of independence and separation. In contrast, unity with diversity welcomes difference. In response, welcoming difference now becomes the lens for spiritual exploration.

In light of the above, unity with diversity can be understood through the metaphor of a *patchwork quilt*. A patchwork quilt is created by stitching together unique and sometimes colour-clashing pieces of cloth. Each piece of cloth retains its uniqueness within the design, yet the overall effect is one of a vibrant and wondrous new creation. In a similar manner to a patchwork quilt, interconnectedness through unity with diversity enables us to connect more deeply to one another, while at the same time continuing to cultivate our unique experience of personal and collective wholeness. Knowing ourselves to be part of a greater whole, enables us to break through and transcend the boundary of competition with *the other*. In turn, judgement, fear, and prejudice dissolve.

The principle of interconnectedness through unity with diversity, requires a certain joyful humility. With joyful humility we can recognize we are not the centrepoint on which Life turns. At the same time, neither are we insignificant to the process. We do have a meaningful role to play. Our role continues to change in response to our time and place in Life's creative *dance* of being and becoming. In terms of our era, both Hubbard and Berry maintained that we humans have evolved to the point where we are now called to be "co-creators" in the evolutionary process. Therefore, rather than simply being

we are not the centrepoint of Life,
yet we do have a meaningful role to play

receptive to, or observers of, the evolutionary process, we are now called to take up a positive agency role. We will however, only be able to ascertain our agency role after we have first located our collective identity within the greater whole of Life itself. Time will tell whether or not we are called to be co-creators in the evolutionary process. One thing we do know at this time is that our current *way of being* in the world seems to be actively working against Life's creative *dance*.

Is this principle actually new?
It could be argued that the grounding principle of interconnectedness through unity with diversity, is actually ancient rather than new. First Nations peoples across the globe have held a similar principle. So, is this principle new or not? The principle is both ancient and new. How? In today's context such a principle is situated within a science-based, system's view of evolutionary history. As a result, those of us who are exploring our *way of being* within such a context, will engage with the principle in a new way to us. As such, we moderns are required to listen to, and learn from, the wisdom of ancient civilizations. At the same time, we cannot simply take their sacred narratives for our own. To do so would be cultural appropriation. So, in the spirit of interconnectedness through unity with diversity, we moderns are required to undertake our own work of discerning a sacred narrative for ourselves. Such a sacred narrative will be grounded in the principle, yet contextualized within our current cultural world view. Harkening back to the *patchwork quilt* metaphor, we moderns are required to weave our own piece of cloth, which may then be stitched into the greater patchwork of human being and belonging.

The grounding principle of a new song of belonging is interconnectedness through unity with diversity.

a new set of assumptions is emerging

A new set of assumptions

Within the light of a systems view of evolutionary history, and the principle of interconnectedness through unity with diversity, a new set of assumptions is emerging. A new set of assumptions will give rise to a new consciousness. A new consciousness can generate a new sacred narrative. Why is a new consciousness necessary? Theoretical physicist, the late Albert Einstein contended, "a problem cannot be solved by the same consciousness that caused it." Therefore, what is required is a new conscious that draws from a new set of assumptions. The following assumptions are breaking into our collective awareness:

A greater Story of Life
The assumption of a greater Story of Life addresses our experience of belonging at the transpersonal level of human consciousness by way of responding to the spiritual questions: "Where did we come from? and "What is our purpose?" We come from and belong within a dynamic 13.8-billion-year Universe Story. Within such an awareness we recognize that Life itself is the principal character and we humans are significant, yet support characters. Within such a view, we realize that our human species is but one unique manifestation of Life itself. Consequently, our purpose is to participate within the awe inspiring dynamic process of Life itself, which is forever and continually in the making. When we locate our identity and purpose within a greater Story of Life, our inner orientating reference point is naturally recast.

An integral framework - giving rise to the human tradition
A systems view has given rise to an integral framework for considering ourselves and the world we inhabit. An integral framework takes into account evolutionary history as a whole, and as such is an all-inclusive view, where each part is necessary to, and included within, the whole. An integral framework has given rise to the notion of the human tradition. The human tradition spans across time from ancient civilizations till the present. Also, the human tradition situates all of humanity in the evolutionary process of being and becoming. As such, the human tradition takes into account human history as a whole, including religious and spiritual traditions. Therefore, the human tradition draws from the rich tapestry of wisdom, beliefs, knowledge, values, and myths which have accumulated within human experience from ancient times until the present. As well as taking into account previous understandings, the human tradition also transcends that which no longer resonates in the present context. As a result, we are able to integrate the wisdom of bygone eras, beyond wholly accepting, or wholly rejecting, the belief systems in which the wisdom teachings originated. Therefore, the human tradition offers a new lens for the way we view ourselves. Such a lens enables us to locate our experience of being and belonging within the wider human community.

Earth is now a place to call home

photo by Andrew Twining

Death is no longer viewed as an enemy
Death is now known to be a natural part of the process of Life itself. Therefore, death is no longer denied, or, viewed as an enemy to be conquered. Such an understanding does not contravene the sense of loss and grief connected with death. It does however, reshape where we place our energies. Rather than placing our energies on conquering death, we place our energies into authentic living.

Earth is now a place to call home
As a young Christian, I remember singing hymns at church about one day going home to heaven; home to an *other place* community. Life on Earth was simply something we had to pass through, before we made it home to heaven. In contrast, a new assumption locates home here on planet Earth. Earth is now a place to call home. At the same time, for those traditions which hold a belief in heaven or Nirvana beyond this Life, home on Earth does not disqualify home on heaven. Why? Because Earth and heaven are no longer viewed through an either/or paradigm. So, for those traditions, the paradigm of both/and means home can now be understood as both Earth and heaven.

We are all in this together
When contemplating pictures of Earth taken from outer space, two realizations become clear. The first realization is how tiny the planet is in relation to the wider physical universe. The second realization is the visual experience of no borders; no state borders, no national borders. Land mass is simply land mass. Oceans are simply oceans. Therefore, even though Earth has various bio-regions, and we humans have various national, cultural, and religious/spiritual differences, we all participate together in this one venture called Life.

We can fully embrace our humanity
The former Western cultural sacred narrative was characterized by what Buddhist nun, Sharon Salzberg, named as, "the myth of not being enough." Within Western culture, such a myth solidified within the Christian religious teaching of original sin. The doctrine of original sin maintained that we were each born into sin and as such required salvation through divine intervention. In contrast, a new assumption recognizes that we are enough, in the knowledge that it is enough to fulfill our potential as human beings-within-the-whole, within any given time and place in history. So, rather than spiritual exploration seeking to transcend the human condition, spiritual exploration enables us to fully embrace our humanity. In turn, we can take responsibility for our own beliefs, values, and behaviours. Also, we can live into the words of author, Alice Walker, "we are the ones we have been waiting for." Therefore, from a premise that we are enough, we can fully embrace our humanity, with all its attendant strengths and limitations.

If the new set of assumptions captures the collective imagination, inner change will occur. The new set of assumptions enables us to give an unqualified *yes* to Life, even within the knowledge that the task ahead is immense.

we now know ourselves to be self-in-Life

photo by Anna Twining

A shift in identity

Self-in-Life
In response to the grounding principle of interconnectedness through unity with diversity, and the assumptions drawn from a systems view of evolutionary history, a shift in our collective identity emerges. Such a shift is toward self-in-Life. Through an identity of self-in-Life we each know ourselves to be unique beings, or self systems, seeking personal autonomy in our own right, while also being intrinsically connected and response-able to a greater whole consisting of systems within systems.
For example: each unique human being is part of a family tree, a local community, a religious/spiritual/philosophical tradition, a cultural world view, the human race, the wider Earth Community, the planet Earth, the Solar System, the Milky Way Galaxy, the Universe, and perhaps even multiverses. To locate our identity within a greater whole of Life itself in this way, we know ourselves to be self-in-Life. Such a shift stands in stark contrast to the former sacred narrative, where the collective identity was one of Self and life, with the emphasis on Self. Within the view of Self and life, we knew ourselves to be separate from, and superior to, the natural world. Now, as we locate our human identity within the new context, we know ourselves to be part of the natural world. Therefore, within an identity of self-in-Life, we know that we each participate in Life's dynamic process that is forever and continually in the making.

The shift in identity to self-in-Life naturally calls forth moral and ethical response-ability. Why? Because when we consciously locate our identity within the systems view of evolutionary history, we can no longer view ourselves as separate, individual beings. In turn, we can no longer live from a values system geared toward individual rights alone. Rather, the view that we are intrinsically part of the natural world, gives rise to a values system geared toward the flourishing of all life forms. Therefore, this new identity in-and-of-itself calls forth personal and collective moral and ethical response-ability.

A shift in identity toward self-in-Life naturally calls forth moral and ethical response-ability.

a new sacred narrative
will stitch together multiple belief systems

A new sacred narrative

We have gone as far as we can go with the assumption that we humans are the centrepoint of Life. So, drawing from the grounding principle of interconnectedness through unity with diversity, the assumptions as listed, and an identity founded in self-in-Life, a new sacred narrative will locate our experience of identity and purpose within the greater whole of the Universe Story. In turn, we will be able to fully embrace our humanity-within-the-whole. Such a notion will break through and transcend the assumptions of anthropocentrism and individualism which characterized the former sacred narrative. As we fully embrace our humanity-within-the-whole, we will know ourselves to be unique beings in our own right, each engaging in our personal *dance* of being and becoming, while at the same time knowing that our unique being is intrinsically connected within and response-able to a much wider web of relationships. Such a view will connect us more deeply to ourselves and to one another, while at the same time enabling us to continue to participate in Life's *dance* of being and becoming.

Furthermore, drawing from the grounding principle of interconnectedness through unity with diversity, a new Western cultural sacred narrative will include multiple storylines, or belief systems, each consciously drawing from the new set of shared assumptions. So, rather than particular beliefs being the basis of a new sacred narrative, it will be the shared assumptions which orientate the differing belief systems. Therefore, much like a *patchwork quilt*, a new sacred narrative will include multiple belief systems stitched together to make a wondrous, creative, beautifully designed cultural experience of being and belonging. A precedence for such a patchwork quilt view was set by lecturer and author, Shireen Morris. Morris argued that three stories made up the Australian identity. The three stories are: the First Nations people, the British colonial settlers, and the immigrant settlers. Each of these stories are unique in their own right while also being part of the whole of the Australian identity. In a similar manner, a new cultural sacred narrative will enable each of the sub-groups within Western societies to remain unique in their own right, while also consciously participating within the whole. For example: each of the theistic, pantheistic, and atheistic traditions which practice within Western culture, would pose their spiritual questions within the light of the new set of assumptions and also the beliefs of their historical tradition. They would, in turn, generate a belief system which rings true to both the new set of assumptions and their historical tradition. In this way, a new cultural sacred narrative will break through and transcend the principles of domination, separation, and independence which grounded the former sacred narrative.

In light of the above, a new sacred narrative will give rise to a new values system beyond the flourishing of the individual, or privileged groups, alone. A new values system will seek the flourishing of all life forms. In this way, a new values system will break through and transcend the former assumptions of tribalism, white supremacy, capitalism, and consumerism.

A new sacred narrative will be generated in response to the new grounding principle, the new set of assumptions, and the new identity.

uniqueness is not sacrificed in favour of the whole

A new song of belonging

A song of belonging involves a visceral experience of connection within self, community, and the deeper rhythms of Life itself. What shape does a new song of belonging take within the context of a systems view of evolutionary history, a shift in identity toward self-in-Life, and a grounding principle of interconnectedness through unity with diversity?

> We belong, simply because we are here.
>
> We belong, as part of a greater whole.

We belong, simply because we are here

A new song of belonging is shaped by the understanding that conditions within Life's *dance* of being and becoming were sufficient enough, and required, that we humans come into existence. Therefore, we belong, simply because we are here. In this way, belonging is a given.

When we consciously locate our personal, cultural, and species' identity within a greater Story of Life, we realize that we can fully embrace our humanity, with all its attendant strengths and limitations. Such a re-turning of our experience of belonging toward humanity-within-the-whole animates our daily living. We experience wonder, joyful humility, gratitude, trust, and reverence for the mystery of participating in Life's creative *dance* of being and becoming.

We belong, as part of a greater whole

As we allow the identity of self-in-Life to permeate the depths of our awareness, we see that our very *being* sits within a much wider web of relationships. Therefore, we each belong as part of a greater whole. Even so, uniqueness is not sacrificed in favour of the whole. Rather, uniqueness is required, welcomed, and celebrated within the whole. As a result, we belong as unique beings in our own right; we belong as unique cultures in their own right; and we belong as a unique species in its own right. Each of the aforementioned categories of human being and belonging are also intrinsically connected and response-able to the wider Earth community. Within such an understanding of self-in-Life, we realize that each one of us does have meaningful role to play in the *dance*.

> A new song of belonging involves fully embracing our humanity-within-the-whole.

to walk humbly within the Earth community,
with wisdom and compassion

Why bother?

It is no easy task to change our cultural *way of being* in the world. So, why bother undertaking the sacred work of recasting our human identity? Well, we humans continue to injure one another; are stripping Earth of its resources; causing pollution of air, land, and oceans; and are stagnating in terms of spiritual wellbeing. Is this the kind of world we want to pass on to our children, our children's children, our children's, children's children? Therefore, for the sake of both present and future generations, change is required. Yet, without a change in our *way of being*, there will be no significant change our *way of living* together. If we were to locate our identity within a greater Story of Life we could experience a new song of belonging in the present. Also, we could live out of a values system which enabled us to walk humbly within the wider Earth community, with wisdom and compassion. In so doing, we could participate in generating a healthy world for present and future generations.

Why is the generation of a healthy world our problem? Surely, Life can take care of its own affairs. It did so for billions of years without human intervention! Well, it would seem that we are at a point in evolutionary history where we humans do impact Life's creative *dance*. The impact of our current *way of living* is even calling into question the viability of a habitable planet Earth in the future. Therefore, as well as living from a values system which seeks equality for all people and life forms, we are charged with the response-ability of participating in Earth's regeneration. Such is our collective purpose at this time. The question remains, "Will we respond to the Call?" Presently, many governments and big businesses are playing at the edges of outer change. While this is a welcome start, the deeper work of recasting our identity is required.

There is one additional reason why we would bother to consciously engage in the work of inner change. The winds of change are squalling beyond, among, and within. So, change is on its way, no matter what? We can choose to deny it, fight against it, or participate in generating change toward a new values system. We can choose to participate in changing our collective identity and purpose, or succumb to the ravages that change will heap upon us. It is our choice! So, the question becomes, will we collectively choose to engage in inner change, or wait until circumstances force our hand?

Undertaking the work of recasting our identity will enable us to fulfil our collective purpose in this chapter of evolutionary history.

in our era, internarrative dialogue is a necessity

Internarrative dialogue

A new Western sacred narrative will include multiple belief systems drawing from a shared set of assumptions, and grounding principle of interconnectedness through unity with diversity. Also, a new Western sacred narrative will stand within the global context of multiple sacred narratives. Therefore, internarrative dialogue is an imperative. Author and founder of Diologos, William Isaacs, contended that dialogue is, "a conversation with a centre, not sides." In relation to internarrative dialogue, *a centre* means that we all participate in a shared reality. Furthermore, when we gather together for dialogue, we gather first and foremost as one human community. At the same time, *not sides* means that there are multiple sacred narratives within the one human community. No one particular sacred narrative takes precedence over another. All life affirming sacred narratives are both required and welcomed within the vibrant *patchwork quilt* of human spiritual wellbeing.

Remembering that unity with diversity welcomes difference, internarrative dialogue enables each participant involved to attune to one another, or in the words of educator and author, Parker Palmer, "to truly see and hear each other." Such attunement does not mean that participants have to agree with each other's beliefs. Rather, as participants listen and respond with nonjudgmental curiosity and respect, each will experience what author and clinical professor of psychiatry, Daniel Siegal, named as the, "resonance" of "feeling felt." Siegal argued that such a *resonance* generates, "an environment of trust." Within an environment of trust, participants can figuratively *walk around* in each other's sacred narratives, without fear of losing their own.

In light of the above, the intention of internarrative dialogue is more than a simple pooling of ideas, opinions, and beliefs. Rather, the intention is to cultivate an environment of connection and trust between people who hold divergent belief systems. Be warned though! Internarrative dialogue is not all sweetness and light. Internarrative dialogue can be confronting, causing inner turmoil within participants. Therefore, authentic internarrative dialogue is a rigorous endeavour. Why? Because internarrative dialogue can raise into conscious awareness previously unrecognized blind spots. So, while the intention is not to change one another's view, internarrative dialogue can give rise to transformative shifts in each participant's understanding of their own sacred narrative. Therefore, internarrative dialogue can evoke inner change.

Internarrative dialogue generates an environment of trust, even among people of divergent belief systems.

A Summary of Changing our Being

Our Western cultural *way of being* in the world has hit a boundary that demands change. In turn, our *way of being* no longer offers meaning and belonging. Also, our *way of being* actively works against Life's creative *dance* of being and becoming. But all is not lost; transformative shifts can occur at such times. In response, the Call of the era - grounded in the symbol of the twisting, turning, singular pathway of the labyrinth - invites us to change from the inside . . . out. Such change involves a transformation of the grounding principle, and assumptions, which orientate our experience of being and belonging; our experience of identity and purpose.

The process of inner change requires that we pose our spiritual questions within the light of current understandings of the origins of the universe, and the nature of reality. Such understandings set the context for spiritual exploration. Today's context involves a systems view of evolutionary history. Within such a framework of understanding, the grounding principle for our *way of being* in the world is: interconnectedness through unity with diversity. The assumptions which orientate our sense of being and belonging include: a greater Story of Life; an integral framework, giving rise to the human tradition; death is no longer an enemy; Earth is a place to call home; we are all in this together; we can fully embrace our humanity-within-the-whole. In response to such a principle and assumptions, a new identity is one of self-in-Life. Self-in-Life gives rise to a new purpose which involves participating in the regeneration of planet Earth, through a values system which seeks the flourishing of all life forms. In turn, a new song of belonging is shaped by the understanding that we belong, simply because we are here. Also, we belong, as unique beings who live in relationship with a greater whole.

Within the understanding that we belong in relationship with a greater whole, internarrative dialogue is an imperative. Internarrative dialogue generates an environment of trust. In turn, an environment of trust cultivates an ever-deepening experience of interpersonal connection, even between people of disparate belief systems.

Concluding remarks

What does it mean to be human in an evolving universe? As far as we know, we humans are the meaning making creatures of the evolutionary process. We have a self reflexive intellect which both drives and enables us to give meaning to our living and our dying, and to experience belonging in our world. We experience meaning and belonging through a belief system, in the form of a sacred narrative, which attunes to the particular Call of the era, and resonates with a majority of minds and hearts of a given society. A life affirming sacred narrative becomes a present moment inner shelter of belonging within Life's creative *dance* of being and becoming. When a sacred narrative is coherent with an era, the people experience a song of belonging. Therefore, the sacred work of being human within an evolving universe entails taking up our place of belonging within a given era.

Change is a natural and necessary part of the evolutionary process. Today's era is crying out for change in the *way we live* together, toward a more equitable world for all life forms. Yet, the structural change required cannot take place without a change in identity. Therefore, while the Call of the era is toward structural change, the deeper Call is toward a change in our *way of being* in the world. Why? Because who we know ourselves to be determines both our experience of belonging, and the way we live within and act upon our world. For this reason, the Call of this era is one of seeking change from the inside . . . out. Such a change involves the reintegration of our human identity within the greater whole; a whole which includes the human tradition, the wider Earth community, and Life's evolutionary *dance* of being and becoming.

Human identity is orientated around the current knowledge and beliefs regarding the origins of the world, the nature of reality, and the human place of belonging within such understandings. In terms of Western culture, identity has been founded on a machine-like view of evolutionary history, and the grounding principles of separation independence, and domination. Such an identity has run its course of usefulness. Consequently, that identity no longer offers a song of belonging, neither can it generate the structural changes required. The good news is that it is possible for Western societies to recast their human identity through embarking on an inner adventure of spiritual exploration within the light of a systems view of evolutionary history. Within a systems view, the nature of reality is viewed through the lens of relationship, and the grounding principle is interconnectedness through unity with diversity. Within such a context, Western societies can locate their identity within the notion of self-in-Life. In turn, their new song of belonging can be shaped by the understanding that they belong as part of a greater whole, simply because they are here. A new identity of self-in-Life founded on the principle of interconnectedness through unity with diversity, will give rise to a values system which seeks the flourishing of all life forms.

To be the change we want to see in the world, requires that we change our *way of being* in the world.

Postscript

What is spirituality?
Within the confines of this book, the term *spirituality* refers to the personal and collective experience of belonging. As such, spirituality responds to the common human longing to belong. Spirituality concerns the three interrelated dimensions of belonging, that is, the intrapersonal, the interpersonal, and the transpersonal. Therefore, in response to our longing to belong, the intention of spirituality is to discover a personal and collective song of belonging within a greater Story of Life itself. When we experience belonging in this way, we figuratively *come home* to ourselves-in-our-world. In turn, we live daily life with integrity and authenticity. Thus, spirituality draws from, and flows back into, daily life.

Present day spiritual exploration toward a new song of belonging will be grounded by the new principle of interconnectedness through unity with diversity, the new identity of self-in-Life, and the new assumptions as listed previously in the book. It is possible for such spiritual exploration to take place within the belief systems of existing religious traditions. But what of the rising number of people within Western societies who identify as *spiritual but not religious?* One new frame of reference for spiritual exploration is that of evolutionary spirituality. Evolutionary spirituality is emerging into a belief system in its own right; a belief system already orientated around the new grounding principle, the new identity, and the new set of assumptions. So, spiritual exploration toward a new song of belonging is not limited to a particular belief system. The one overriding criteria, however, is that a belief system remain open to a life affirming experience of belonging-within-the-whole.

The language of spirituality
The language of spirituality is poetic. *Poetic* here refers to metaphor, imagery, and symbol. As such, the language of spirituality is open to various layers of meaning, beyond the literal explanation of the words. Poetic language enables sacred narratives to both form and evolve within an open belief system. Open belief systems are responsive to the Call of the era, and can change when necessary. On the other hand, when the language of a sacred narrative becomes literalized, the narrative takes the form of dogma. *Dogma*, here refers to a closed belief system which is viewed as the one and only, forever truth. Dogma can give rise to fanaticism and fundamentalism. Closed belief systems are the antithesis of a life affirming sacred narrative which is responding to the Call of the era.

Spirituality in relation to other disciplines of human endeavour
What is the relationship between spirituality and the three disciplines of philosophy, psychology, and the sciences? *Philosophy*: spirituality takes into account the wide range of philosophical responses to existential questions. At the same time, spirituality goes beyond the intellectual understandings of philosophy, to the experience of belonging in response to such understandings. *Psychology*: spirituality takes into account the wide range of psychological theories and therapies which focus on a healthy self concept within community. Spirituality, however, goes beyond a healthy self concept within community toward an experience of belonging within a greater Story of Life. *The sciences*: spiritual exploration takes place within the light of current science-based knowledge and beliefs regarding the nature of reality, as well as the workings of the world and the human body/mind. Even

so, spirituality goes beyond knowledge about the world, to a life affirming experience of belonging in the world. Thus, spirituality is not a stand-alone discipline. Rather, spirituality both includes, and transcends, the disciplines of philosophy, psychology, and the sciences. Consequently, spirituality is the sacred work of being human with in an evolving universe.

Spirituality entails both intention and practice. In line with the intention of discovering a song of belonging within a greater Story of Life, what does spiritual practice involve? At this point in Western history, spiritual practice no longer focuses on living on some plane of existence beyond the human condition. Rather, present day spiritual practice enables us to fully embrace our humanity-within-the-whole. It is important to note that an attitude of nonjudgmental curiosity and lovingkindness is essential when engaging in spiritual practice. Such an attitude enables each person to fully embrace their unique *way of being* in the world, without attachment to a fixed identity. Two helpful spiritual practices for our era are:

Contemplative self inquiry. Contemplative self inquiry engages us in our personal transformative *dance* of being and becoming; our inner adventure of self discovery-within-the-whole. The practice enables us to drop beneath the confines of our constructed self concept. Then we can perceive inner wisdom's stirrings toward personal wholeness, in the form of an *inner shelter of belonging*. Engaging in the practice of contemplative self inquiry enables us to figuratively, *stand in our own ground - openheartedly.*

The ongoing practice of contemplative self inquiry *turns on* posing open ended questions, and the corresponding affective experience which arises in response. The practice involves expressing, exploring, discerning, integrating, and celebrating inner movements toward an *inner shelter of belonging*, and dissolving counter movements. As such, contemplative self inquiry may well involve identity formation, shadow-side integration, a process of forgiveness, and conscious grieving. Because contemplative self inquiry involves an ongoing practice of allowing spiritual questions to work their way through to completion, it can be helpful to journal responses along the way.

Meditation. Meditative practices enable us to notice our affective experience, without totally identifying with it. When we no longer totally identify with our affective experience, it can become an entry point for perceiving inner wisdom's stirrings. Furthermore, meditative practices enable us to experience the deeper rhythms of Life itself. Such deeper rhythms are not experienced as an empty void, but rather as the dynamic and creative energies of: 1. love, in the form of an ever-deepening experience of communion with self, and with a wider web of relationships; 2. faith, in the form of being able to give meaning to our living and our dying, at any given time and place in history; 3. hope, in the form of the possibility of transformation, which is grounded in reality. Meditative practice may include the more classical meditation forms, or simply sitting quietly in bushland. Meditative practice may also include movement. For example: mindful walking, yoga, or tai chi.

For more on the life affirming spiritual practices of contemplative self inquiry and meditation see: www.treeoflifespirituality.com

About the author

I am a female human being, born in inner suburban Melbourne, Australia. As a non-indigenous woman, I live on the lands of the Wurundjeri people who are the traditional custodians of this land and waterways. As such, I write from and into a non-indigenous Australian Western cultural context; a context which shapes my sacred narrative of being and belonging. I was also born at a time when the Christian religious tradition was central to that cultural world view, although there were signs of that being on the turn. While Melbourne is where I have lived my entire life, I have travelled numerous countries and experienced a variety of living styles and belief systems. Also, as evidenced in this book I like to play, usually via Adobe Photo Shop, with photos taken on my phone. I am often stunned by the outcome. I choose to include pictures with my writing because images can resonate with the deeper, unlanguaged parts of our inner being. Therefore, images can hold and sustain us during times of spiritual exploration when no words are sufficient. Also, images continue to resonate when words have long passed out of memory.

Even though pictures are an important part of my work, I also spend much time seeking words which give expression to, and integrate, the inner transformation taking place within me. Until now, I have chosen to post my writings on the website: Tree of Life Spiritual Practice Education for Today's World. This was in preference to writing a book. Why? Because the notion of bookending the ever-evolving insights and understandings of my inner travels seemed an absurdity. So, what changed? Well, I am noticing the inner stirrings of a turning; the seeds of something new are commencing to break open in the dark, fertile soil of my new song of belonging. As such, it seems appropriate to gather together the insights and understandings gained through this season of my living. Therefore, I have chosen to write my little book of big ideas.

I founded Tree of Life Spiritual Practice Education for Today's World in 2007. Since that time, I have facilitated workshops for the general public and professional development sessions for accredited spiritual companions, both locally and internationally. Presently, Tree of Life comprises an online resource for people seeking to explore and deepen their song of belonging. The Tree of Life approach to spirituality is grounded in contemplative principles and practice based on the three pillars of: 1. an attitude of rational curiosity which embraces a gentle, open, playful, receptive spirit of inquiry, and reflection on lived experience; 2. spiritual exploration within the light of current knowledge and beliefs regarding how the world came to be/continues to be; 3. the practice of authentic living, drawing from a values system which seeks the flourishing of all life forms.

Respectfully,
Kaye Twining,
Tree of Life - Spiritual Practice Education for Today's World
www.treeoflifespirituality.com

Resources

The following authors are tall timbers, so to speak, in terms of pioneering cultural transformation. Their writings caught my imagination. In turn, my reflection on their research both shaped and challenged me into my current thinking:

Christina Baldwin, Storycatcher: Making Sense of Our Lives through the Power and Practice of Story (2005)
Nora Bateson, Small Arcs of Larger Circles: Framing through other Patterns (2016)
Thomas Berry, The Great Work: our Way into the Future (1999)
    The Dream of the Earth (1988)
Brene Brown, Braving the Wilderness: The quest for true belonging and the courage to stand alone (2017)
Fritjof Capra & Pier Luigi Luisi, A Systems View of Life: A Unifying Vision (2014)
Bruce Chatwin, The Songlines (1987)
Pema Chodron, The Wisdom of No Escape and the Path of Lovingkindness (2013)
Brian Cox, The Human Universe (2014)
    The Wonders of Life (2012)
Charles Eisenstein, The More Beautiful World Our Hearts Know is Possible (2013)
    Climate: A New Story (2018)
Duane Elgin, The Living Universe (2008, 2010)
    Promise Ahead: A Vision of Hope and Action for Humanity's Future (2000)
Scilla Elworthy, PHD, Pioneering the Possible: Awakened Leadership for a World that Works (2014)
Yuval Noah Harari, Homo Deus: A Brief History of Tomorrow (2015)
Barbara Marx Hubbard, Conscious Evolution: Awakening the power of our Social Potential (1998)
Anne Hillman, Awakening the Energies of Love: Fire for the Second Time (2008)
William Isaacs, Dialogue: The Art of Thinking Together (1999)
Sameet M Kumar, PH.D, Grieving Mindfully (2005)
Satish Kumar, Elegant Simplicity: The Art of Living Well (2019)
Bernard Lonergan, Method in Theology (1971)
Steve McIntosh, Integral Consciousness and the Future of Evolution (2007)
Joanna Macy & Molly Young, Coming Back to Life: Practices to Reconnect our Lives, Our World (2014)
Shireen Morris, Radical Heart: Three Stories make us One (2018)
James O'Dea, Cultivating Peace: Becoming a 21st Century Peace Ambassador (2012)
John O'Donohue, Eternal Echoes: Exploring our Hunger to Belong (1998)
Diamuid O'Murchu, Quantum Theology: Spiritual Implications of the new Physics (1997, 2004)
Parker Palmer, On the Brink of Everything (2018)
Bill Plotkin, Nature and the Human Soul (2008, 2017)
Robert E Quinn, The Deep Change Field Guide (2012)
Daniel Seigel, Mind: A Journey to the Heart of Being Human (2016)
Sebene Selassie, You Belong: A Call for Connection (2020)
Bob Stilger, After Now: When we cannot see the future where do we begin? (2017)
Shunryu Suzuki, Zen Mind, Beginners Mind (1970)
Vimala Thakar, Glimpses of Raja Yoga: An Introduction to Patanjali's Yoga (1991, 2005j
Daniel Christian Wahl, Designing Regenerative Cultures (2016)
Alice Walker, We are the Ones we have been Waiting for: Inner Light in Times of Darkness (2006)
Ken Wilber, Integral Spirituality: A Startling New Role for Religion in the Modern and Post Modern World (2006)
Margaret J Wheatley, So Far from Home: lost and found in our brave new world (2012)
David Whyte, CD - A Great Invitation: The Path of Risk and Revelation (2013)

Copyright 2021

Except where indicated, the photos in this book were taken by the author. Where indicated, photos were taken by members of the author's family, and used with their permission. All pictures are copyright and not to be used without permission from the author.

In terms of the written word, the way the ideas are presented in this book is unique to the author. The ideas, however, emanate from the *spirit of the age*. Such ideas are, and belong in, the public domain. Consequently, the ideas cannot be copyright. Therefore, as long as quotations from this book are referenced to the author, and used to further the global conversation regarding the Call of the era to change from the inside . . . out, quotations may be used without permission.

 A catalogue record for this book is available from the National Library of Australia

ISBN: 978-0-6452715-0-8 (paperback)
ISBN: 978-0-6452715-1-5 (ebook)

Photo descriptions

Front and back cover
Leaves fallen to the ground at the Melbourne Botanical Gardens, Victoria.
The clarity of each leaf's colour and shape was heightened by intensifying the contrast setting. For me, autumn leaves beautifully represent the natural, ongoing process of inner change.

Pioneer
Redwood Forest, East Warburton, Victoria.
The forest is quite small and there were many visitors that day. Even so, my husband Andrew and I were able to find a quiet spot away from the crowds. I took off my shoes so that the skin of my feet could feel the ground beneath. I sat in the stillness of the moment, taking in the Stillness.

Table of contents
The Great Smoky Mountains National Park, Tennessee, USA.
The original photo of me walking on a path in the Smoky Mountains, is overlaid with a Photoshop cosmos pattern. The photo acknowledges that my work on inner change follows a pathway which was set in motion, but not set in stone, by earlier pioneers of the inner change process. Also, the picture represents the recasting of our human identity within a greater Story of Life itself.

Introduction
Lake Sanatorium, Macedon Ranges, Victoria.
The day was damp and misty. There is something alluring about trees in the mist. The prominent trees in this picture had stunningly smooth, whitish trunks, revealed by the old layers of bark falling away. This picture represents something of the process of inner change, in that the freshness of a new sacred narrative of being and belonging is revealed, only as the outer layers of a now obsolete sacred narrative fall away.

What is the Call?
Venus Bay, Victoria.
The photo is overlaid with a Photoshop wallpaper effect. The photo represents something of the joyful abandon, reverence, and trust that can be experienced when embracing our unique human place of belonging-within-the-whole.

Responding to the Call
Photo 1. Cradle Mountain-Lake St Clair National Park, Tasmania.
The photo represents an *inner shelter of belonging* within Life's creative *dance* of being and becoming. Without such an *inner shelter*, we could become lost in the vastness and mystery of the *dance*.
Photo 2. Suburban Northcote, Victoria.
The photo is of a beautiful stained glass panel set within a front door of a home. The photo is overlaid with a Photoshop freeform effect. The photo represents the inner disorientation which can take place when a once meaningful *home of belonging* breaks apart.

Recognizing the season
A Japanese maple tree, place unremembered.
I am particularly struck by the brilliant colour of the leaves, and the way the light plays on them. Yet, these stunningly beautiful leaves will fall and become compost for the soil below. The photo reminds me that our meaningful cultural sacred narratives cycle through seasons of change, in a similar manner to the Japanese maple.

The Call and truth
Boston ivy in our suburban backyard.
This ivy began as a small shoot, but has grown over the years. Now the ivy threatens to take over the fences and walls of our home! I have played with the colours through Photoshop. The photo represents something of the subjective and objective nature of truth, in that the leaves are fact, yet the colour is an interpretation of the fact.

The Call of this era
Lake Sanatorium, Macedon Ranges, Victoria.
The background of the photo was softened to heighten the clarity of the green fungus. The green of the fungus symbolizes new life. *New life* here refers to a new sacred narrative of being and belonging. The circular form of the fungus symbolizes wholeness, the non-linear nature of transformation, and the sacred work of inner change. *Sacred* here refers to attuning our human longing to belong with Life's Call of the era. The formless centre symbolizes the deeply held assumptions which orientate our human identity. It is such deeply held assumptions which require change.

A summary the Call of the era
A cropped section of a lily flower, in a vase of lilies on our kitchen table.
The colours have been enhanced to further draw out the shape of the petals in contrast to the shadows. The gently curling petal symbolizes that our longing to belong sits within a gentle Call of belonging within the deeper rhythms of Life itself.

Change is a given of life
Photo 1: Autumn leaves on the ground at Melbourne Botanical gardens.
Photo 2: The Boston ivy again.
Both photos are taken in the autumn. The leaves are changing in colour, before they drop from the trees. Autumn represents the season of change.

A lexicon of change
Photo 1: I bought this sculpture many years ago. The photo is overlaid with a Photoshop paper effect and a water colour effect, to enhance the sense of flow and colour. For me, the sculpture symbolizes the personal dance of being and becoming, which in turn sits within the greater dance of Life itself.
Photo 2: The backyard of a home on the Mornington Peninsula, Melbourne.
The photo of the butterfly is overlaid with a Photoshop pattern effect to soften its overall look. The photo is a reminder of the overall process of a caterpillar turning into a butterfly. Such a process involves the form of the caterpillar turning to mush within the cocoon, before the imaginal cells can start to shape the new form of a butterfly. Even so, the butterfly is not a better form to that of a caterpillar. They are both unique expressions of Life itself. In a similar manner, at certain times in history, a once meaningful cultural sacred narrative necessarily turns to mush, before a new sacred narrative can emerge.

The winds of change are squalling
R.J. Hamer Arboretum, Olinda, Dandenong Ranges, Victoria.
The photo is overlaid with the Samsung Pen and Wash style, to accentuate a sense of relentless movement.

Opening the door to inner change
Photo 1: The Lavender Farm, Daylesford, Victoria.
The photo symbolizes that while we cannot force or control the process of inner change, we are required to consciously open the door to the possibility of inner change.
Photo 2: A lake near Jasper, Canada. This photo represents Quinn's assertion that we undertake the deep work of transforming our inner assumptions without knowing the duration or final destination. Therefore, as Quinn argued, "we build the bridge as we walk on it."

Photo 3: R.J. Hamer Arboretum, Olinda, Dandenong Ranges, Victoria.
The original photo was softened by the Pastel filter on the Samsung smartphone, to reduce its clarity. The photo symbolizes that even though inner exploration has no predetermined pathway, a pathway is cleared by the posing open ended questions.

Conscious grieving
A gumnut in a suburban street in Melbourne.
Conscious grieving involves numerous feelings and bodily responses beyond that of tears. Even so, the stillness and clarity of the water drops on this gumnut, symbolizing tears, reminds me that conscious grieving is purposeful and life affirming when undertaken within the spiritual practice of contemplative self inquiry, within the gentling light of lovingkindness.

Impediments to inner change
A common daisy, in our suburban garden.
The colour of the original photo was inverted through Photoshop, so that the petals are visible, but not their full range of colour. The photo signifies that inner change is possible, but not a given.

A summary of the nature of change
The parklands of Bundoora, Melbourne.
In terms of the symbolism of trees, O'Donohue wrote, "Letting go of old forms of life, a tree practices hospitality towards new forms of life." (*Eternal Echoes: Exploring our hunger to belong*).

The labyrinth: a symbol for inner change
A finger labyrinth currently adorning a wall of my study.
The photo is overlaid with numerous Photoshop effects, to symbolize the opaque nature of the inner venture toward transformation. As symbol, the labyrinth continues to remind me that even though the *dance* takes many twists and turns, there is but one pathway into the centre and back out again. Also, the labyrinth symbol continues to remind me that the inner spiritual venture flows from, and returns to, the shallows of daily life on the other side of the deep. Therefore, the focus of spirituality is living daily life with integrity and authenticity.

Facing the limits
Photo 1: The parklands of Bundoora, Melbourne.
The stark, dry, prickly, dead thistle bush is symbolic of the way our current human *way of being* in the world is causing the death and extinction of numerous plant, fish, and animal species within the wider Earth community.
Photo 2: A public rally for social justice in the central business district of Melbourne.
The photo is overlaid with a Photoshop effect, to keep the visual effect of many people, without revealing the identity of any particular person. The photo represents the desire of many people to seek social justice, but whose protests are ineffective because there is no cultural change in identity which can support significant social change.
Photo 3: Mount Martha, Victoria.
The photo is overlaid with a Photoshop cosmos effect. The photo of a tree with one trunk and multiple branches signifies that a new cultural sacred narrative will of necessity embrace multiple belief systems, each drawing from a shared set of assumptions.

The good news
Federation Square, Melbourne.
I took the photo one day when I was sitting in an enclosed part of the square between shops. I happened to look up and was captivated by the beauty of the criss-cross roof. The colour of the photo was played with, to draw out the contrast between the dark lines within the colourful background. The photo signifies the beauty, complexity, and interrelatedness of a systems's view of evolutionary history.

Grounding principle of a new context
Photo 1: An inner suburban garden.
The various features of this Australian yellow Waratah flower represents the notion of unity with diversity, which both welcomes and requires difference.
Photo 2: The multiple leaves, with their varying colours, signifies that within a new cultural sacred narrative, we humans are not the centrepoint of creation. Rather, in a similar manner to the autumn leaves, we are unique beings, who have a meaningful role to play within the whole.

A new set of assumptions
Photo 1: A bush, commonly known as Chinese Lantern, growing in our front garden.
The photo signifies the breaking through of a new set of assumptions which can orientate a new cultural sacred narrative of being and belonging.
Photo 2: Keppel Lookout, Marysville, Victoria.
The photo represents that Earth is now a place to call home.

Shift in identity
Wilsons Promontory National Park, Gippsland, Victoria.
The photo underscores the notion that within an identity of self-in-Life we are not outsiders, simply observing Life. Rather we know ourselves to be unique beings who can observe, even as we are intrinsically connected and response-able to Life itself.

A new sacred narrative
A daisy in a suburban garden in Melbourne.
The darker markings around the centre of the daisy make it look like the individual petals of the plant have been stitched together by a thread. This photo underscores the way that multiple belief systems can be figuratively stitched together into a cohesive whole, around a centre of shared assumptions.

A new song of belonging
A Chinese Lantern flower in our suburban front garden.
The background of the photo has been softened, to heighten the brilliance of the flower. This photo is the delicate and beautiful flower which has blossomed from one of the buds pictured at the commencement of the section on Changing our Being. The photo of the individual flower underscores the notion that uniqueness is not sacrificed in favour of the whole.

Why bother?
Sanatorium Lake, Macedon Ranges, Victoria.
The human figure is dwarfed by the huge tree trunks close to him. But rather than feel insignificant, the feeling is one of awe and humility for participating in such a wondrous evolutionary process.

Internarrative dialogue
A magnolia flower in our suburban front yard.
The photo is of a cropped section of a magnolia flower, whose colour and texture were manipulated, and then mirrored and repeated through a Photoshop collage effect. The photo represents an environment of trust which can be generated when participants truly engage in internarrative dialogue.

A summary of changing our Being
The parklands of Bundoora.
The colour of the photo is changed through a Photoshop effect, emphasizing the way the light plays with the bark of the trunk. The photo underscores both the beauty and the wildness of engaging in the transformative *dance* of changing our cultural identity.

Concluding remarks
The front garden of a suburban street.
The photo of the sunflower and bee, both fulfilling their role within Life, leads me to wonder if we humans will be able to find our own *way of being* part of the whole, at this time in history.

About the author
A tree at a place unremembered.
The photo has been played with in Photoshop to accentuate the gaiety and vibrancy of Life.

Resources
The Redwood Forest, East Warburton, Victoria.
It seems somehow fitting that this book both commence and conclude with a photo from the Redwood Forest. Regarding forests, author and poet, Robert Louis Stevenson wrote: "it is not so much for their beauty that a forest makes a claim upon our hearts, as for that subtle something, that quality of air that emanates from old trees that so wonderfully changes and renews a weary spirit." The quality of air in the Redwood Forest certainly renews a weary spirit. This final photo catches something of the grandeur of the tall trunks enveloped with their leafy canopies, reaching towards the light of day. The photo symbolizes the tall timbers, so to speak, who have shed light on the path of being the change in the world, through changing our *way of being* in the world.

embrace the *dance* of being and becoming

www.ingramcontent.com/pod-product-compliance
Lightning Source LLC
Chambersburg PA
CBHW041427010526
44107CB00045B/1527